Advanced Prai

"Down to earth, heartfelt, _____ _____, ____ wise. In **Soaring Through Setbacks** *Cheryl Perlitz does a terrific job of reminding us that we have much to learn from nature and each other. She has a knack for inspiring even the non-outdoors people to explore more of the outer world, and for encouraging everyone to explore deeper within."*
-**Matt Baron** Columnist/ Journalism trainer freelance writer who has done work for Time and the Chicago Tribune

"Thank you, Cheryl, for sharing from your expertise, your heart, and your soul. With the valuable, real-life lessons you share in this book, everyone can learn new ways to soar above the obstacles and losses in their life."
-**Barbara Glanz, CSP** (Certified Speaking Professional) Author of *Care Packages for the Workplace, Care Packages for the Home*, and *Balancing Acts*

*"***Soaring Through Setbacks** is an authentic guide for those who have been detoured from life's course by tragedy, disappointment, and loss. Cheryl's authentic personal experiences and helpful tips provide navigational assistance to create an empowering new course filled with reassurance and hope."
-**Barbara Haag**, RN, MS Director of Women's Health Services/ Perinatal Grief Counselor and author of *Clinical Practice Development... Using Novice and Expert Theory*

"Cheryl is a true heroine; her experiences and insights will help everyone soar through life's transitions. Her passion, enthusiasm and honesty are contagious."
-**Jim Mahoney** Vice President of Retail and International Sales, Bondo Corporation

"*Cheryl Perlitz's straightforward book opens your mind and inspires your heart. Her life-story, metaphors of mountain climbing, and survival tips will help you discover how to recover from grief, loss, and change with insight, vision, and purpose. It is a guide to help you move from the 'valley of grief and loss' towards the 'summit of victory in recovery.'*"

-Christine Corelli, speaker/trainer and author of *Wake Up and Smell the Competition*

"*Cheryl has written the book this world needs. If your life has fallen apart, this book will give you the insights, help, and encouragement to put it back together. Cheryl's wisdom and compassion bring hope to the hopeless and a sense of direction to the lost.*"

-Rita Emmett, author of *The Procrastinator's Handbook* and *The Procrastinating Child: A Handbook for Adults to Help Children Stop Putting Things Off*

"*Cheryl reveals a remarkable approach to handling life's setbacks, whether it's the passing of a loved one, separation or divorce in a relationship, or the loss of a job. Filled with real-life examples, Cheryl shares her step-by-step passage from the 'wilderness of grief and uncertainty' to the 'summit of peace and fulfillment,' and gives the reader a roadmap for turning life's stumbling blocks into stepping stones.*"

-Loie Evans, author and publisher *Westwater Books River Guides* Mountain trekker, wilderness adventurer

"*I would recommend this book to my students, colleagues, and friends. Cheryl shares a vision for living and sharing life that is true and heartfelt. Her humor and insights are infectious!*"

-Father Paul E. Carrier, S.J. PhD. University chaplain, Fairfield University, Fairfield, Ct

Soaring

Through Setbacks

Rise Above Adversity
Reclaim Your Life

Cheryl Perlitz

04 05 06 07 HH 10 9 8 7 6 5 4 3 2 1
First Edition
Printed in the United States of America
ISBN: 0-9745824-1-7
Library of Congress Control #: 2004105771

SEL031000 Self-Help/Personal Growth/General
SEL010000 Self-Help/Personal Growth/Grief

Cameo
Publications
PO Box 8006
Hilton Head Island, SC 29938
1-866-372-2636
info@cameopublications.com
www.cameopublications.com

To all who are trying to find their way out of the wilderness of grief and uncertainty. My prayer is that your path will lead to the summit of peace and fulfillment.

To my two Toms...

Tom Perlitz, who shared the first half of my life with me as my best friend, lover, and father of our three great boys;

and

Tom Marquardt, who is my new soul partner. Together we have passed through the valley of widowhood and have climbed the mountain to new life. We are blessed to have found joy again with each other.

Contents

Acknowledgments

I feel so incredibly lucky to be alive and joyful. For a while I didn't think I could function another day. I was blessed to have gone through a process that taught me how to live: the process of change and transition known as grief. I learned how to design my life as a climb up a mountain, to take charge of my life from the inside out, to design my responses to challenges as calls to adventure, and to look at life from outside the comfort zone. I feel profound gratitude to those who have helped me along the way.

I have my boys to thank for all of their loving support, albeit in different ways. To Tommy, my oldest son, I am grateful for the guidance you have given to all of us in helping us to stand on our own feet as a family. Tommy, his wife Erin, and their three daughters Ellie, Sarah, and Katie are the light of my life. To Doug, I am thankful for your spiritual presence and support... especially for the example you have given all of us in living a life of charity as you work with the street kids of Haiti. I love our moments of silence together at the bookstore with a large latte in hand. To Chris, I am grateful that you share your gentle and yet adventurous spirit to all of those whose lives you touch... and make us smile.

To Bill and Gloria Perlitz who embody unconditional kindness and generosity. Our family could never have made it without you. I am also grateful for the support of Carol Heitman Mazzocco, my "sister" who has dedicated her life to helping children and families deal with cancer. Thank you to Father Paul Carrier, who has become a confident, spiritual guide, and proxy family member. He always supports us through the big family events: funerals, weddings, christenings, and adventure trips. Also, my three brothers Peter, Chris, and Tim Heitman have always been there when I needed them.

To my wonderful old friends, especially Jane Varley and Tricia and Will Hagenah, who I grew up with since I was six years old. You were always at my side, no questions asked, no matter

how stupid I acted. To Dick and Barbara Cardinal, special trea-
sured neighbors and friends. To Carol Born, who stuck with
me through all the ups and downs. To Marjory and Tom
Goettsche, Alice Lewis Pickett, and Nancy Moksczycki, my
special laughing friends who look at life through the refreshing
eyes of humor every day. What a gift they have!

To Susie Morrison Meyer, my special soul sister, who is my
mirror image in every way. You were a surprise gift given to
me during my toughest times. Your positive attitude and love of
nature and adventure remind me how lucky we are to have
mountains to climb.

To Janet and Jim Frieberg, dedicated Christians and spiritual
guides who ALWAYS were there for emotional and spiritual
help. You taught me about compassion and unconditional love
and have mastered the art of listening and making "the heart
connection."

To my tennis buddies, my new friends who quickly worked
their way into my heart with kindness and sweet new friendship: Joyce Knauff, Sally Kaulas, Louise Yao, Karen Balsbaugh,
Sue Melciorre, Sharon Farrell, Sue Cole, and Nancy Donahue.
What great people you are and SO MUCH FUN!

To my buddies from Steamboat Springs, Colorado, especially
those amazing strangers I met who became instant friends. To
Lynn and Bill Davis and the whole Whittemore family, especially Stan Whittemore, who at 85 has gone through two major
losses and STILL lives life with gusto. You teach us all how to
grow old with grace and style. To KC and Keith Casson, who
taught me how to cook and encouraged me through the whole
writing of this book with treats and laughs. To Gabe Butler of
Montana Log Homes, who built me a perfect little nest loft that
became my writing place. I could never have done it without
the inspiring view of the mountains to spur me on, and those
cool mountain breezes coming into my new window.

To my ski club buddies who helped me figure out how to be a
single person again: Jim Hemminger, John Lemm, Don and Lynn

Sullivan, Joan Galantha, and Bill Walsh. To Judy Johnson, my fantastic supportive "girl friend" who helped me look at life through new eyes.

To my friends and mentors in the kick boxing class. To Kathleen Jeffreys, a real YES person who oozes positive energy and encouragement in everything she does. To Cindy VanZelst, a sweet mom of four who demonstrates an innate ability to make the "heart connection." And to Richard Daniels, who is an ageless man with lots of energy. You stand in the back row, in a room full of women, with a gleam in your eye and a smile on your face.

To my NSA (National Speakers Association) friends, Barbara Glanz, Rita Emmett, and all the wonderful people in the Illinois chapter who have taught me to have enough confidence to be able to share my life with my wonderful clients. A special thanks to Christine Corelli, who was always willing to help me through my literary and business dilemmas, Cyndi Maxey, and Lori Klinka. Together we are the gruesome threesome. Also to Joe Contrera and my mentor Mike Wynne, who helped me to get out of my own way.

To Tom's children, Susie and Peter Ohlandt and Tommy and Julia Marquardt. You have accepted me into your dad's life unconditionally, unselfishly, and with great love. You have also provided me with two wonderful grandsons. Especially I thank Erich Marquardt, who has become a great friend and computer consultant. You have made our lives fun, active, and alive with energy.

I especially want to thank Dawn and David Josephson from Cameo Publications for giving life to my words. They were great to work with and made writing this book beyond fulfilling and gratifying for me. I truly value your professionalism and patience and feel blessed to have you as my partners and friends.

George Foster, my cover designer, was a delightful gift. Another great guy to work with who was able to capture the essence of my book with amazing graphic design. Thanks George!

THE CLIMB

For Barry Evans ~ By Megan Weber Hogan

It is the climb that strengthens us
To go onward.
Life is mountains and valleys,
The struggle to go upward
And the freedom
Of height.
It is the courage
To persist,
To climb,
To dedicate self to the challenge
And attain
What was pursued,
The view from the top.
The never ending moment of
Strenuous confusion
About
Where to place the foot next,
Is forgotton
When the whisper
Of the
Mountain
Pulls us to the peak.
It is then that we see
More mountains,
More valleys
And realize
We can never stop climbing,
Never stagnate
In stillness.
Then we catch
The momentary glance
Of what life is
It is the climb,
The exhilarating, never ending climb

This poem was written as a tribute to Barry Evans, a gentle young adventurer who moved on from this life at 15. Barry's friend, Megan, described him as a 'fantastic soul' filled with a joyful, enthusiastic spirit. Megan wrote this poem as a way of coping with her own emotions and of trying to understand the concept of death. She is now a wife and mother of 2 boys.

Preface

"Life is full of mountains to climb. . .Those mountains become vehicles for wonderful new beginnings."

— **Cheryl Perlitz**

Many people have asked me, "Why did you write this book?"

My answer is simple: I wrote this book because one like it didn't exist when I needed it. I wrote this book for the people I saw browsing in all the bookstores I went to for six years. I wrote this book for those readers who went directly to the grief and self-help aisles and flicked through every book on grief, recovery, and self-help. Every one of them had "that look" in their eyes—one of being lost and dazed. After spending hours leafing through books, they would occasionally buy one ... but usually they just stood, reading a few pages here and there.

◈ I saw the widow, just like me. She stood in the grief aisle every night like a lost bird not knowing where to go next.

◈ I saw the young mother carrying her young son. The child tried to smile, but inside you could see that empty look—the one that says, "Daddy isn't coming home." The mother smiled shyly, tears in her eyes.

❖ I saw the older man who carefully sidled to the business aisle when he saw me approaching, only to return to the self-help aisle again and again, "just to take a look." He was clearly lost and bewildered. I ran into him for many days in a row and then again five months later, when he was in the business aisle. This time his demeanor was clearly different. He seemed taller, more confident. I asked him if I would be seeing him in "self-help" again. "No," he said, "I got a job."

❖ I saw (in the media and in person) all the people who suffered a loss after the Twin Towers collapsed on 9-11, as well as those who lost someone in the Iraq war. I saw all those people who never had closure to their relationships.

After six years at bookstores, I saw them all. I knew what they were doing in the self-help aisle, because I was doing the same thing. We were all looking for the same thing: Answers to life's most complex questions. "Why do bad things happen to good people?" and "Where do we go from here?"

Before we go any further, let me make one thing perfectly clear. I'm not a trained therapist. Rather, I'm a common person, like you. I make that distinction because bad things happen to people like us. We don't need to hear theories of the *id* and *ego* or complicated explanations about the process of grief. *We need to know that we are all in this life together, and that we will experience major changes along the path of life.* We need support and encouragement. We need acknowledgement to help us feel better, to get rid of those awful feelings of pain, and to make sense of it all. We want to feel that *just maybe* what we are feeling at those times is normal … that we *can* survive and be okay…and that this, too, shall pass.

But mainly, I wrote this book because it has been bubbling up in me for seven years, and I knew if I didn't write it, I would regret it. I wrote it for that passion inside that had to come out, or I would implode. After all those years of perusing the aisles of bookstores and libraries, and all the searching, I learned one important truth that I will share with you in the following pages:

> Life is full of mountains to climb, and they are challenging and painful. At the same time, they are full of adventure and almost always teach us lessons that we must learn. If we have an idea where we want to go, prepare for survival, step out of the comfort zone, face the obstacles in our path, throw the rope for help, and persist through the final push, those mountains become vehicles for wonderful new beginnings.

Your new beginning starts now.

~ **Cheryl Perlitz**

Part I
Surviving

"Grief and the deep, slow process to which it yields have a rhythm of their own, and to refuse to sink into those rhythms is to make a monument of a past which no longer has a future." — **Robert Romanyshyn**

Chapter One

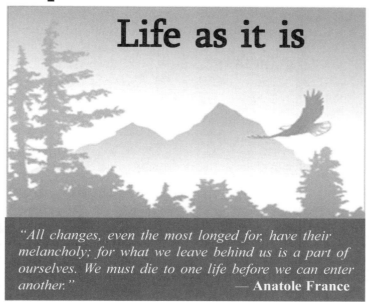

Life as it is

"All changes, even the most longed for, have their melancholy; for what we leave behind us is a part of ourselves. We must die to one life before we can enter another."
— **Anatole France**

Life is predictable ... at least I had always thought so. We perk along day-by-day, hour-by-hour, doing the very best we can. For the most part, life goes as expected, with only a few glitches along the way. We encounter irritants we can handle, and then we move on. We are walking along, zigging and zagging, and then ... the mountain appears.

I **always thought that**...If we eat right and take care of ourselves, we would be healthy. We may get sick occasionally, but we will be generally disease-free and fit. **BUT SUDDENLY the MOUNTAIN APPEARS**...and we get **REALLY SICK**.

I **always thought that**...If we do our best at work, show up on time, do what is expected of us plus a little extra, we will be rewarded. If we get along with our co-workers, we will have healthy relationships at work. If we contribute to the company's bottom line and financial success, we will be appreciated. **BUT SUDDENLY THE MOUNTAIN APPEARS** ... and we **LOSE OUR JOB**.

I always thought that... If our country does the ethical things, with good intentions based on humanitarian needs, we will be safe and secure. **BUT SUDDENLY THE MOUNTAIN APPEARS ...** and we are thrown into financial instability and our **FREEDOM AND SECURITY ARE THREATENED.**

The truth is, change is always happening. As soon as we think we have life all figured out and we know where we are going and how we will get there, a mountain appears in our path and we must look at life differently.

When My Own Life Fell Apart

I was securely entrenched in the suburban life. My husband, Tom, was a corporate 'Type A' hard working man, and I, a small business owner, running my business from home. Our daily life revolved around supporting our three boys in college. Occasionally we were able to find a break in the routine and throw our two large dogs in the back of the Suburban and take off to the forest preserve for a run. The end of the day was never really the end of the day. A quick dinner was always followed by more work from home. We were able to sneak an occasional respite from the routine with a trip to the mountains for hiking, biking, and adventuring.

Our dream was to get our children "launched" and then move to the mountains we loved in Steamboat Springs, Colorado. We were building a little log cabin on top of the mountain. Unfortunately, our dream was never to be.

We had just returned from a wonderful weekend with our youngest son, Chris, with whom we had celebrated Tom's fiftieth birthday. Tom and Chris ran together in a 10K race on a tedious up and downhill course in Boulder, Colorado. Our first day back from Boulder, Tom felt fluish and complained loudly, as he always did when he was sick. I was away all day on business but checked in on him frequently. When I returned home in the early evening, he said he felt like he needed to go to the hospital. I'd heard that before, like when he had a red mark on his arm and thought he had gotten Lyme disease, and when he skate boarded into a parked car and thought the black and blue mark was an indication of a hemorrhage that was rapidly moving towards his heart.

Instead of rushing to the emergency room, we called the doctor. Tom explained his symptoms, and the doctor gave us the typical response: "Drink lots of liquids, take two aspirin, and call me in the morning." When I arrived back home from a quick trip to the local grocery store, Tom reported that he was feeling better. When I checked on him twenty minutes later, he was dead.

The autopsy showed he did not have a heart attack, but died of myocarditis, or inflammation of the heart caused by a virus.

The boys received the dreaded phone call that night and were on planes home from their various campuses the next morning. Everyone's reaction was different: one oblivious (me), one angry, and the others devastated with sadness. We marched through the next few days in a fog, with me showing no emotion at all, and them feeling sadness and shock in their own private ways.

The traditional dark, haunted day of Halloween was the day of the funeral. It was a rainy cold day, and the church was packed. Along with personal friends, business friends, and acquaintances from all over the world were representatives from the Make a Wish Foundation, Children's Memorial Hospital, and several other charities Tom served loyally as a board member. Some of our neighbors spoke and with tears in their eyes and wobbled through their own tributes. A standing ovation brought a final end to a life well lived! John Denver singing *Rocky Mountain High* sent us off to Colorado and Tom's final resting place.

The next morning at six o'clock, the four of us were on our way to scatter Tom's ashes in the mountains of Steamboat Springs, Colorado. We all wore one of Tom's hats, representing his various personalities. There was the "Elmer Fudd" hat with earflaps that he wore when he cut the lawn, the ski hat, the baseball hat, and the cowboy hat with the feather hatband. Looking like a sad version of The Village People, we went through the baggage claim. In a backpack, in a $3.00 plastic container, were Tom's ashes.

When the inspector said, "We're going to have to look in the backpack," and then "I'm going to have to look in the black box," we all looked at each other with expressions of shock. I piped in, "That's only my husband," and handed him the death certificate. The inspector took the box to the supervisor, holding it at arm's length, and then returned it to us. In the plane, instead of putting Tom in the overhead, we passed him around between the four of us.

Once safely on the ground, we made the three-hour drive to Steamboat in a rental car in a blinding snow storm. We then went up to the top of Buffalo pass, sliding, teetering on the edge, and bumping on a dirt road full of boulders and pot holes. Finally, we arrived at the trailhead. After a painful two-hour hike uphill through knee-deep snow, we arrived at the peak. With snow blowing fast and furiously, making visibility nearly impossible, we took handfuls of ash, tossed them up, and let the wind carry them where it willed.

We found out later that Spring that Tom's ashes landed in the middle of a large volcanic rock with an indentation loaded with wild flowers.

Several days later, I arrived at the bank where I met with a lawyer and account manager. After a review of my tax returns for the last two years and the year's bank statements, it became clear I was headed for serious financial challenges.

I had to sell the cars, get rid of the house, and find a way to make a living. Taking it one step at a time, I sold the cars first. The five-bedroom house went next, which I replaced with a studio apartment. Finally I found a wonderful home for my two sweet Golden Retrievers and bid them a tearful farewell.

The next day I left for Prince William Sound where I spent a month kayaking in the beautiful Alaska wilderness, only to be air lifted out of there and back home due to the death of my other best friend – my mom. My new life had a shaky start, but at least I had few things left to lose. I had nowhere to go but up.

Losing What Was and Finding What Will Be

The transition between "what was" and "what will be" includes a period of grief, fraught with emotional agony and keen mental suffering. For most, this period is a rough ride of emotions and struggles. It's a roller coaster through a tunnel that seems to have no end. Whether you've lost a job, a spouse, a child, a pet, a dream of what could be, or your financial security, the grief process is the same. We give up the past—a past that will never be again—and we find a future—a future we are yet to see.

I always thought that grief was a simple process. You feel sad for about a year, and then you get over it and move on. I've since learned that grief is a much longer process than that. When my husband died, I lost not only him, but also my identity, my security, my lifestyle, and my life as it was. My friendships changed, as did my family as I knew it. The grief process I went through will always be a part of who I am.

While losing a spouse is difficult, **losing a child is a much more devastating loss.** It goes against the natural order of things ... the way life should be. We're not supposed to outlive those we bring into the world and nurture. When you lose a child, you lose not only part of yourself, but also your dreams for the future. The family is forever different for the loss and pain it goes through together. That child and the pain of losing that life will always be part of who the family is and will become.

Losing a job means losing much more. For many, losing a job means losing your reason for existence—who you are and what you live for. Many people agree that a job is more than "just a job." Our career is who we are, where we spend our time, and how we value our own self-worth. In a way, losing that identity is a death of who we are.

Along with the loss of identity comes the loss of financial means. We must find a way to survive without that monetary security. Those people with whom we have spent so much time are no longer a part of our lives. Only a rare business relationship survives the jolt. Feelings of betrayal, loss of trust, and disrespect remain. Retirement by choice, quitting, or losing a job against our will all mark an end of the old and the start of a new path.

The bombing of the World Trade Center on 9-11 was a loss far greater than anyone could have imagined. Aside from the loss of life, we as a nation lost our sense of security, our financial stability, and our privacy. The event forced us to rethink our policies and take a close look at our government and our relationships with other countries. It also caused many to examine their religious convictions. Our dreams of a peaceful, carefree life were shattered. Our identity, as a nation, instantly changed ... and so must we.

Our dreams motivate our lives. What we think should happen and what actually transpires are often two different things. We want healthy, beautiful, and mutually beneficial relationships, but sometimes that doesn't happen. Or we think we will have a certain kind of life, but we never reach what we strive for. Or we hope for wonderful, kind, loving teenagers, but then they go through their hormone surges and social pressures and turn into independent and sometimes "crazy" people. We then think, "Another dream shattered." **Not having those dreams materialize is death of another kind.**

Every one of the 6.3 billion people on this planet has lost something, from baby teeth to a loved one. Whether we feel the physical pain of the new tooth coming in or the emotional pain of creating a life without a loved one, we know a door has closed in life. We are left standing between the closed door and the one that has yet to open—between the past and the future. Sometimes we are so busy looking at the door that just closed that we miss the one that's opening. Sometimes we see the crack in the new door but hesitate to step through. **Grief is that time between the doors when we are struggling to make the next step.** It's a quiet time, a turbulent time, and a time of indecision. It is the transition between the old life and the new life.

The Mountains

I grew up climbing mountains.

Mountains are beautiful and challenging, majestic and all powerful. They also have lessons to teach us.

Climbing mountains taught me about change. Every mountain has a surprise around the corner, an obstacle in the path, or a storm brewing minutes away. During every climb you find yourself teetering on a ledge, knowing you could fall, and agonizing over the moment of impact.

The drudgery and agony of trudging along step by step taught me the lessons of persistence, patience, and determination. During those times, nature provides wonderful treasures to keep us interested as she fills our hearts with wonder and awe … a glacier around the next bend, a few mountain goats teetering, a beautiful sunset.

No matter how challenging a physical mountain is, **the hardest mountains we climb are the ones we can't see.** They are the ones life throws in our path, when things are humming along smoothly. Those are the mountains in my life I am the most proud of scaling.

Surviving the mountain of grief that came after my husband's death was difficult because it wasn't tangible. It was a mentally tormenting climb that seemed to have no end and no assurance of survival. The path was solitary and personal. To survive that kind of climb—and live to tell about it—is a real accomplishment.

Sometimes we are climbing several mountains at once. That's when many aspects of life seem to crumble simultaneously. For example, when we have a major health problem, life as we knew it changes. Poor health is followed by fear of pain, loss of the dream for a long and healthy life, loss of freedom, and emotional and financial stress on the family. They are all mountains to climb.

The process of climbing real and unseen mountains is the same.

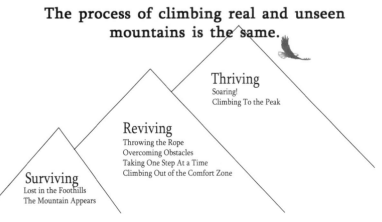

Thriving
Soaring!
Climbing To the Peak

Reviving
Throwing the Rope
Overcoming Obstacles
Taking One Step At a Time
Climbing Out of the Comfort Zone

Surviving
Lost in the Foothills
The Mountain Appears

Surviving

At first we try to survive … **only to survive.**

Then the mountain appears, and we are initially shocked, sometimes mad, and usually in denial. We don't want to climb the mountain, but we know we must.

We feel lost in the foothills, and until we are able to become emotionally stable, this is where we need to stay as we attempt to find ourselves again. At this time, we strive to find our footing so we can move on and prepare to climb.

Reviving

Once we have our footing, we prepare and make the climb to new life.

We visualize the peak and have some idea where we are going and what we want our life to look like. This is when we plan our route.

Next we prepare for survival. We can't climb a mountain if we are not physically and mentally prepared. Preparation is getting ready to do our best and persist through the tough times.

As we prepare, we must lighten the load. We travel further and faster if we carry a light load.

Maintaining an adventure attitude helps us persist. Attitude is a personal choice. The adventure attitude looks at mountains as an adventure and opportunity for positive change.

As we take risks, we step out of our comfort zone. Finding a new life is all about the painful stretches that lead to new things.

We take one step at a time to get there. It involves sweat and struggle, but we travel day-by-day, hour-by-hour, step-by-step and make progress.

We handle obstacles along the way. We know we will always encounter unexpected obstacles along the path. Those challenges make us stronger and teach us many lessons. We get stronger with every obstacle we meet, greet, and defeat.

We throw the rope to others along the way. The support and help of friends, family, and strangers we meet along the way helps us attain success.

Thriving

Thriving is the final stage. Our life's purpose becomes clear.

As we climb to the peak, we make that final push to the top, which connects us to a world larger than ourselves. The lessons we learned along the way made us stronger.

In the end, we soar above the mountain; we are free-spirited and compelled to share the lessons we learned and help others.

Seasons of Change

Nature has always been my solace and my teacher. In nature I found answers to many of life's biggest questions, such as "Who are we?" and "What is our place in this big world?"

Nature shows us a world of perfect symmetry. Life is followed by death, then new life and then death again. Seasons change constantly like a circle spinning in the same direction. A sense of balance assures the survival of all creatures in total interdependence. Change is predictable and constant and works the way it should. It is an ongoing process that never ends, and we, as humans, are all part of it.

Unpredictable changes sometimes interrupt nature's cycle, yet the cycle continues. The cycle we see in the change of seasons is a metaphor for our personal reality. Seasons come and seasons go, just as mountains come and mountains go. In our lives, darkness is always followed by light, and then the darkness reappears. In fact, if we never experience darkness, we wouldn't know the light. We let go of old results in new beginnings and renewal ... and then we must let go again. Struggle is followed by joy ... and then more struggle. If we didn't struggle, we wouldn't know joy.

The seasons and cycles of nature are part of our lives, part of our years, and sometimes part of our days. We may start the day fresh and new (summer). We have a bounce in our step and are on top of the world. Then the unexpected happens and we go right back into winter, struggling to regain that fantastic feeling of new growth in spring and the full light of summer.

The funny thing about the seasons is this: When you are in one, even though you secretly want things to change, you somehow don't believe the next season will ever come. It's as if your brain shifts you into a new gear, and that's where you stay. Summer comes in and grabs you by the heart, and that's where you are. Winter comes and rolls you into a ball, and you go into yourself and stay there. Then, things amazingly change, the spring comes, and you exhale again.

The ancient philosophy of Taoism in China, Mongolia, and Tibet uses metaphors of nature to define the systems of philosophy, medicine, and society. They believe the cycles of nature are dependent upon the elements that make it up (i.e.: metal, wood, water, fire, and earth). These five elements fit into a continuous cycle that repeats itself and creates harmony in the environment. They divide the cycles into five growing seasons where objects, people, and nature are in harmony. They are:

The Chinese Seasons

Autumn
- Letting go of what was
- Giving up control
- Grief and Pain
- Confusion
- Acknowledgment

Late Summer
- Gathering
- Awakening
- Connecting with others
- Appreciation
- Grounding
- Nurturing

Winter
- Assessing Resources
- Deep Listening
- Discovery = What's Inside
- Deep Inquiry
- Meditation

Summer
- Playfulness
- Loving Life
- Living in the moment
- Joyfulness
- Communicating

Spring
- Making Future Plans
- Learning
- Seeing Possibilities
- Seeing - Vision
- Setting Goals
- Having Hope
- Having New Energy

Autumn

In Nature

Autumn is a season of great beauty and vibrancy as the leaves become full of color and then finally fall. It's as if nature needs to show itself with gusto before its ultimate decline. The days become shorter and the growth hormones in animals and plants decrease as life slows down. In some ways, autumn is also an active period in nature. Squirrels store food so they can use it later, bears fatten up so they have the energy to give birth and nurse their young during winter, and trees store the food and energy reserves needed for next spring's growth. Seeds scatter so life will begin again in the spring. All of this happens to prepare for the winter period to come.

For Us

For people, autumn comes when we age and life gradually changes. We slow down, and our priorities change. Our bodies, energy level, and actions no longer define us. In the autumn of our lives, our old selves are released to prepare for the older and wiser selves we are yet to be.

For me, autumn came when my husband died and when I had to abandon my home-based business. These times stripped away my self-definition, as a wife and manager, in order to prepare for a new stage of life. I had to go inside, acknowledge my situation, let go of what I no longer could have, and accept the situation at hand. Autumn is our period of grief and loss.

As a Nation

Autumn came when terrorists attacked the World Trade Center and shook our sense of security. Our beliefs in how the world viewed us and how we viewed others were in question. We had to challenge many of our old beliefs and go deep into our roots to redefine our values and priorities.

Autumn is a Time For

◈ Pruning and stripping away the old to make way for the new.

◈ Breathing deeply, giving away control, and focusing only on those things we can control.

◈ Experiencing the grief and the pain that goes with change.

◈ Acknowledging what is and appreciating the cycles of life.

Winter

In Nature

Winter is the time to slow down and regenerate from the inside out. Bears go into hibernation, while trees go into a state of dormancy. Both rely on the food resources they stored during the fall.

For Us

Winter chases us inside. In the winters of our lives, the loss of "what was" forces us to find new meaning. This is a time to reevaluate who we are and what we are about. For example, after a job loss, the shock of rejection is followed by a need to figure out what we want in life, how we can get what we need, and where we want to go next. It is the time for assessing our resources so we can make a plan.

As a Nation

After 9/11, the winter was a period of deep questioning. As a nation we asked, "Why?" "Why us?" and "What now?" We experienced feelings of grief and emotional exhaustion combined with an urgency to figure out the answers to universal questions. Life had handed us a roadblock. We began realizing that:

◈ We are not always in control of what happens to us. How can we regain control?

◈ Life is not supposed to be like this. Why has this happened?

◈ We must continue living. But how?

◈ We're different than before. But who are we now?

◈ We must do something! What direction do we go?

Winter is a Time For

◈ Deep inquiry.

◈ Assessing resources.

❖ Deep listening.

❖ Discovering what's inside.

Spring

In Nature

In spring, life emerges from the cold of winter with new life. But before nature becomes beautiful with new growth, it goes through the period of mud and muck. The earth that was frozen in winter melts into a muddy mess, but in this mud, the conditions for rebirth exist. The muck sends rich nutrients back into the earth to make it fertile for new growth.

Spring comes tentatively and erratically with storms and unsteady temperature changes. As the days lengthen and the sun rises higher in the sky, the temperatures rise, triggering change in plants and trees. Hormones are released that regulate plant growth. We see the first crocuses and snowdrops show themselves, and **HOPE IS RENEWED AGAIN**. New life is coming.

For Us

Spring is a season of hope and new life for us also. The diligent introspection and gathering of resources during the winter period finally starts to bear fruit. It's as if we now know who we are and are ready to show it. As a widow, I experienced spring when I was finally able to say, "I am whole and fine just the way I am." For me it came when I finally knew I could make it on my own. I was no longer defined as a "widow," but as "me."

With a job loss, spring is the period of understanding your strengths, what you want out of life, and making a plan. It's the time when you grow in a new direction, and the growth comes fast.

As a Nation

Today, we are still going through the winter period. However, spring will come when we redefine ourselves outside of the context of the present threatening environment. It will come when we envision a peaceful resolution to the Middle East conflict and plant the seeds for a new life of peace and harmony around the world.

Spring is a Time For

❖ Planting the seeds for new growth and making plans for the future.

❖ Honing skills and learning new ones.

❖ Seeing potential and possibilities.

❖ Setting goals and seeing vision.

❖ Being enthusiastic and appreciating the gift of new life.

❖ Having hope.

Summer

In Nature

Summer is the season of plenty—a period of abundance when all of nature works together to create what is needed. This is the time when trees bear fruit and when the forest fills with undergrowth and new life. Plants grow rapidly because of long days and optimum sunlight. The reality of fall and scarcity of winter are long gone as new growth begins.

For Us

In summer, we find we are finally on our way. We grow tall and strong and in a new direction, and release the energy we have stored through fall, winter, and spring. Summer is a period of thriving. It is a time to appreciate and to live in the moment. Summer is a time of loving where things are, and living congruently with one's goals and values. The job searcher finds the path is set, and success is here. This is the time when all the hard work of letting go, assessing resources, deep inquiry, and having a vision results in success. It's time to enjoy the new energy of doing and being what you love.

As a Nation

Post World War II brought unprecedented prosperity and the birth of the baby boomers. The number of jobs increased. Loans were cheap and easy to come by. The end of gas rationing brought cars to the road. New suburban communities changed how people lived, and the supermarket changed the way people shopped. Innovation and stepped up production met the increased demand for products. The "American Dream" was exported by efforts such as the "Friendship Train" and Marshall Plan. As a nation, we basked in the newfound prosperity of summer.

Summer is a Time For

◈ Playfulness.

◈ Loving life as it is with a fresh new attitude.

◈ Living in the moment.

◈ Joyfulness.

◈ Communication.

◈ Celebration.

Late Summer

In Nature

Late summer is the time of harvest. During late summer, the new growth has come to maturity and is ready to be gathered and savored. Plants bear fruit and animals are fat and happy. The intense activity of spring and summer slows down.

For Us

"Gathering" happens in late summer for us, too. It is the time to gather up the fruits of our growth and spread them around. We do this by sharing what we learned and gained through the seasons, with friends and with those in need. Just as nature creates abundance, so do we when we come together in community. For me, late summer requires me to use the lessons I learned through the grief process to help others in the depth of it. Likewise, the person enjoying abundance in his job is able to approach his work life with a broader understanding to share.

As a Nation

The post-war prosperity after WWII led to the awakening period from 1966-1980. Abundance led to space travel, a drug influenced culture, and emphasis on civil rights for all Americans. The GREAT SOCIETY of Lyndon Johnson brought with it Medicare, federal aid to education, and the establishment of the Department of Housing and Urban Development. A society comfortable in its prosperity made way to a society fighting to avoid the reality of the Vietnam War. Autumn was not far away.

Late Summer is a Time For

◈ Appreciation.
◈ Surrounding yourself with excellence.
◈ Awakening.
◈ Connecting with others.
◈ Gathering.
◈ Grounding.
◈ Nurturing.

Nature is continuously teaching us the Greatest of Lessons:

◈Change is Always Happening
◈Trust the Process... You may not have Control
◈Have Patience... Knowing things will Change
◈Live for the Moment
◈Stay Awake... Experience the Season
◈Relax ... Let Life Happen to You
◈See Each Stage as an Opportunity

Chapter Two

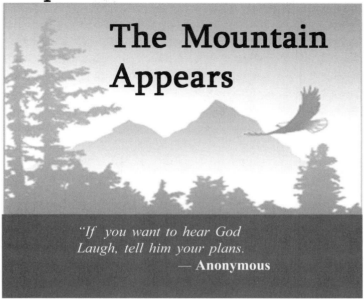

The Mountain Appears

"If you want to hear God Laugh, tell him your plans.
— **Anonymous**

The day my husband died, the life I knew was gone in a split second. Without warning, our life together was part of the past … all of our hopes and dreams, financial security, and our wonderful *Leave It to Beaver* life was gone.

In the four months that followed, both my parents died. I also lost my house, my three cars, and my two dogs. I was robbed, sued, and even had a lady drop dead next to me in the movie theater. I was thrown into total instability, unsure where the next dollar would come from with three children in college. I quickly learned **life was not going to progress the way I had planned.**

I was shocked to learn that bad things could happen to *me*. I couldn't run away or ignore it and pretend it didn't happen. The mountain was there, in my path, stopping me dead in my tracks. I couldn't go around or through it. I had no choice but to climb it if I ever wanted to move ahead with life.

My friend Keith suffered a similar tragedy when he lost his job. He worked for the same company for thirty years and was promoted many times. Then, without warning, his job was gone. The boss he had been so close to called him into the office and fired him. Four months later, when the company went bankrupt, Keith lost his pension, his savings, and his financial security. He had bills to pay and a family to provide for. He lost his entire way of life, his confidence, and his identity. He thought of himself as a failure and was embarrassed to tell others his fate for fear they judge him that way. Worst of all, Keith felt betrayed and lost trust in people.

Keith had a mountain to climb. He had to climb up and over it ... or stay stuck with a mountain in his way.

The River of Life

I can't think of mountains without thinking of the rivers that formed them. The two work together, day-by-day, season-by-season, and have for millions of years. The result is the dichotomy of the river, which is ever flowing and moving and adjusting, and the mountain, which stands strong and tall and is a result of the power the river has imposed on it over the years. The river carves its way through, and the mountains answer with majesty, beauty, and secrets that reveal themselves every step of the way.

Like the river, the grief process is forever moving and changing, shaping us as the water shapes the land it flows through. It is cyclical and changes pace and characteristics by the hour, by the day, and by the year.

The Flow

The water's flow shapes the river, shapes the land, and defines the river's size, as well as its path. It creates pools, channels, and gorges. It also determines the habitat and landscape that surrounds it, the food sources within it, and what animal and plant life can survive in it. The flow reacts to the obstacles in its way and shapes them as much as they shape it. The animals and plants evolve from the river, benefit from it, and depend on it for life.

As it gathers and changes, the river's flow ultimately finds its purpose, which is to feed the thirsty land, contribute to the environment, gather its sources along the way, and bring fullness to a final destination. It becomes a small part of something larger.

In the same way, our own lives flow from our sources to the final destination. **We affect all that we encounter along the way, and we adjust and change until we finally come to a place of final contribution.**

The Undercurrent

The undercurrent is the unseen force that powers the river. Beneath the surface are hidden life, energy, and character. The undercurrent can be strong and drives the flow. It bubbles up and exposes itself when it encounters obstacles in its path.

As we travel along on our journey, our surface hides a whole life underneath. Like the river, we have a hidden force that drives us. We each have a whole life that is vibrant; sometimes it's beautiful, sometimes murky, and sometimes unknown. It bubbles up and exposes itself during turbulent times. When we see what lurks beneath the surface, we discover its true character.

"What is essential is invisible to the eye."
— **The Little Prince,** *Antoine de Saint Exupery*

The Rapids

The rapids show us a bumpy ride. The water changes because of unseen rocks beneath the surface and land obstructions along the way. Grief and change are also challenging bumpy rides and a little frightening at first. At times, we think we can ride out the turbulence, and at times staying afloat seems like an insurmountable task. Amazingly, we almost get used to the turbulence and adapt to it so **it becomes part of life's flow.**

The Waterfalls

Tiny rapids turn into larger ones, followed by a short calm area, and then the waterfall appears. It is strong, powerful, and one of nature's greatest hazards and most beautiful phenomena. To ride a waterfall, we brace ourselves, keep paddling to ensure stability, and go with it.

Waterfalls interrupt the normal flow of life with great force and strength. Sometimes, for no reason at all, we are in an emotional fall, and the intensity of feeling is strong and powerful. Even when we know such an event is coming, we don't feel any better. The emotions are still so overwhelming that we are not sure we will come out of it. The waterfall is unpredictable, intense, powerful, and frightening because we feel totally out of control. The more waterfalls we survive, the more we know we can survive in the future, and the more we value those times. Then we savor the feeling that awaits us when we arrive at the gentle swirling pools at the bottom.

The Whirlpools

The whirlpools form when the rushing water hits an obstruction, such as rocks or canyon walls. The whirlpool turns around and around on itself, exposing the water underneath. This is not a place teeming with life; instead it's the place where life is sucked in and spit out. In the grief process, the whirlpools churn us around, and we come up gasping for breath, changed by the experience. If we fight the process, we only fatigue.

The secret to the whirlpools of transition is to relax, let go, and realize we are not in control of many things. Even though we think we will sink at the time and never come up for air, we eventually pop up, just as a leaf sucked into the whirlpool will pop up automatically. For us, the whirlpool is a time of confusion when we turn around and around, unsure what to do, where to go, who to be with, or what to do next. In fact, if we just let go, the answer will come to us. If we relax and let the river digest us, it will spit us out.

The Pools

Reaching the calm pools is the reward. Those deep, beautiful places along the river team with life we can't see from the surface. Under the surface is a whole world that feeds on what the river brings to it. For us, in transition, **the pools bring those moments of calm and reflection.** This is the place for learning and recuperation. In the pools, we go inside and see what might really be there...and thrive.

The Eddies

Eddies are at the river's edge where the rapids join the slower water of the main current, sometimes backing into a calm pool. The water actually turns around and flows upstream along the bank. The river feeds the land around it, contributing valuable water the trees and animals need for survival. Life on the shore, in turn, reflects its beauty back into the calm water below.

In transition, this is the safe time to flow and reflect on what you've learned and see how far you've come. The eddies are the calm times that transform us into newness. We start to give back and connect with other life around our shores, and the picture becomes more healthy and whole.

To the Sea

In the end, the river, now bulging with life, energy, and fullness, joins with the sea, contributing all it has gathered along the way. **The river of grief, change, and transition is this:**

◆ We flow.
◆ We change.
◆ We grow.
◆ We adjust.
◆ We give back.
◆ We contribute to a greater whole, to each other, and to what we touch.

Emotional Reactions

The initial reaction to the mountain's sudden appearance varies from person to person. We all tend to react initially with gut instincts. Some go into a hole and hide there, some go into denial and try to live life as usual, and some hit the ground running to avoid the pain and move on. Whatever your reaction, it's fine. This is not the time to reinvent yourself or to be someone you aren't. While different, the major emotional reactions are the same, in some ways, for all of us.

We feel life has a different meaning. **We are strangely detached from the world around us,** and in fact don't even feel a part of it. We feel left out. The day my husband died, the news was full of car accidents and people crushed under tractors. Each victim earned a place in the local news. The media called for sympathy for those who died. My first reaction was: "What about me? Shouldn't the whole world be mourning my husband? Shouldn't I get the support of the rest of the world, just like their survivors are getting?"

When a person loses a job, he or she has a difficult time sympathizing with others. After all, it's his or her job loss that is unjust and painful, not anyone else's. At those times, people feel devalued and unimportant. They want to scream: **"HEY WHAT ABOUT ME??!!"**

This is when reality usually hits. We realize the emotional challenge is ours and ours alone. As much as we would like to think our problems are important to other people, they just aren't … at least not in the same way. Nobody can feel the way we feel because they are not in our skin! Some people may say, "I know just what you're feeling," but they don't and never could.

My Comfort - The Comfy Chair

We had our favorite chair in the family room. It was one of those great, comfy chairs that made its way into the heart of the family and the heart of our most comfortable room. This chair lived through a world of family emotions, sitting quietly when we had something serious to discuss, or a marital argument. We sat in it when we nursed babies, waited for a teenager to come home from a night out, or had a major financial discussion. It adjusted to us by providing us with slight indentations that fit our bodies perfectly. When the footrest came up, you felt as if you were sinking into a cozy custom-made feather bed.

This was Tom's favorite chair. Every night when he came home from work he would plop into it before dinner. I would jump onto his lap and we would have a silent hug before I went to the kitchen to finish dinner, or he would go to the computer to slave over the bills.

After he was gone, I went to this chair when I felt sad. Occasionally I would give into the loneliness and sadness. I would make myself a big bowl of popcorn, close the curtains and turn out the lights, and watch the movie Shadowlands with

Anthony Hopkins—the story of C.S. Lewis, who lost his wife to cancer. At the part when he visits his wife as she lay dying … I really let loose. The leather chair would shake and quiver under me as I sobbed as hard as I could until the credits came on. Three days later my puffy eyes finally got back to normal and I felt a little better. Initially I followed this routine about once a week, and then less frequently as time went on, each time finding out anew that I could survive the whirlpool and come up on the other side.

The Value of Humor

I always surround myself with funny people – those who see the humor in everything, including the bad things that happen to us. My friend Nancy was with me after Tom died, and she stuck with me through those painful months after. She is a master at the one-liners and threw them into every situation when the chips were down.

Three weeks after Tom's death, Nancy and I went to the movies to see *Legends of the Fall* with Brad Pitt. At the part when Brad sacrificed his brother's heart to the "buffalo god," I heard a choking sound coming from the seat next to me. Nancy leaned over to me and said, "I think that woman next to you is taking this movie a little too seriously."

A few minutes later, the lights in the theater went on. People looked back at the projection booth, started throwing popcorn and shouting, "Turn off the lights. Turn off the lights!"

I looked next to me, and there, lying on the floor, was that lady. People rushed to her from the back of the theater to help her as she gasped for breath. Nancy turned to me, and out of the side of her mouth said, "I'm never going anywhere with you again!"

I started to laugh. I laughed so hard I could hardly get air. I laughed so hard I started to wet my pants. It was such an inappropriate time for a boisterous belly laugh that I rushed out of the theater into the lobby. I laughed so loud and hard that I thought I would burst. I laughed the rest of the night, and I thought of her comment through the whole next week. It was an incredible emotional release. Certainly I was experiencing the roller coaster.

I often look back at those emotional swings and think about the intensity of it all. At some point in the transition process, I remember someone saying to me, "Well, at least you're feeling," and I suppose that is what it's all about. **Not feeling** is the alternative, and you'd have to be dead to not be feeling (or in need of serious psychological help).

Recently, I talked to a number of people who lost jobs in the financial instability of the post-9-11 economy. One particular former employee of Arthur Andersen, the company that collapsed as a result of questionable tax accounting practices, told me of the betrayal he felt when he lost his job.

As he explained, "My first reaction was anger and bitterness and I wanted revenge ... immediately. This was followed by about four days of sitting in a chair staring into space ... dumbfounded. I finally decided that I was getting nowhere with any of this and had to move. I went through periods of depression and frantic action, until I finally became productive. Now I look back, a year and a half later, and feel grateful that I can do what I always wanted to do. I found a great job in a totally different field. I probably would never have had the nerve to try it if I hadn't been forced to. You asked me how the roller coaster ride changed me. Well, the hills flattened out as time went on. I still feel the ups and downs, but the ride is more predictable and I am really enjoying the ride."

The Role of Anger

Anger sometimes rises from deep inside and wants to lash out at things and people, both seen and unseen. Betrayal leads us to want revenge, while hurt leads us to find something or someone to blame. Through anger, we find a place to put our strong emotions. However, if acted upon, anger can turn on us and become our worst enemy. It can intensify the feelings we are trying so hard to redirect.

When Joe's company went bankrupt, Joe lost everything: his retirement and financial security, his identity, his life. He was angry for several years. But it was important for him to experience those feelings. His anger stalled him right where he was, paralyzed with emotion. It fed on itself and then finally burned out. Had he acted on it, there's no telling what other damage would have resulted—what other hurt he would have caused others and himself.

> *"Anger is an acid that can do more harm to the vessel in which it is stored than to anything on which it is poured."*
> **- Mark Twain**

The Role of Denial

I'm not a therapist. I don't know my id from my ego, but denial has a bad rap. We are taught to think that someone in denial has no touch with reality. The negative connotation is that someone in denial is in need of serious psychiatric help. In truth, denial has a very positive and productive place in the period of transition we call grief and adjusting to change. **Denial is actually a gift.**

Denial is God's bubble, a protected place where you are safe and enclosed. After the shock of change, it's normal to avoid grasping the seriousness and pain of the situation. God somehow provides a protective land to inhabit that gives you permission to get through the change without dealing with the pain. After Tom died, I had financial matters to take care of, a house to sell, dogs to find a home for, a job to secure, and I had to find a place to live. I know I functioned with the day-to-day details of "life after death" only because I had a safe place to be … in God's bubble. Denial was truly my friend.

The bubble gradually faded away. That's when I realized the impact and the finality of what happened. At that point, I allowed myself to feel the pain. It was a gradual process and, little by little, I absorbed it and integrated it into the new life I was trying to start.

The reality check about denial is this: Sometimes it's hard to get past it. Forging ahead with the daily details of life and ignoring the reality of the situation must end eventually. Usually, reality hits after time; however, if that doesn't happen and if:

◈ You never feel the pain,

◈ You remain unrealistic about the situation,

◈ You are unable to move ahead, or

◈ You always focus on the past as if it is the present,

then it's wise to seek professional help.

Physical Reactions

We each have a mind-body connection. The mind controls so much of what the body does. Have you ever noticed how we lose sleep when we have something weighing on our minds? Or, we think negative thoughts and then our whole life turns negative? **The fact is, what we think becomes the reality.**

Adjusting to grief and facing change is truly hard work. In pain, our minds try to work things through, which causes stress. **The emotional stress leads to loss of concentration and light-headedness.** It's hard to sleep. Loss of appetite snow-balls and it becomes even harder to eat. We end up with head-aches and stomach aches. Our immune system weakens, and so we catch colds and flus. We even become more susceptible to dental problems. **Our minds and our bodies cry out for care**, at a time when self-care is the last thing on our minds.

Everyone I interviewed about their grief process said the same thing: They couldn't sleep. Some said they couldn't eat, while others said they couldn't stop eating because they were under such stress. And everyone said they had trouble concentrating.

I thought I was totally in control of myself after Tom died. However, my driving was just horrible. During the transition period, I found myself looking at the road but *not* looking at the road. I thought I was concentrating but I wasn't. I would drive along and then find myself "lightly tapping" the cars in front of me. I must have had a dozen small fender benders. Once I went to a job interview and, while practicing my lines in the car, I found myself sitting in the tennis court parking lot. I was at the wrong location and late for the important interview. I still have no idea how I got there. My head was not as clear as I thought.

All of that sounds scary, I know. And when you think about it, it's amazing people survive the shock of major change. The biggest lesson we need to learn is this: Of all the different changes we go through in our life, going through major grief and transition is the one time when you really need to **take care of yourself.** Give yourself permission to "go with the flow" and pamper yourself if you can. You will make mistakes and do some crazy things, but that's part of the deal. It's all part of a life that is changing, and you are surviving the river of life.

Survival Tips

 ❖**It's okay to be mad,** but think long and hard about acting on your anger! Burning bridges behind you and causing others pain is non-productive and could come back to bite you some day. Let the feelings pass and move out of it.

❖**Let yourself feel fully and completely.** It's okay to go through a roller coaster of emotions. In fact, it's totally normal if you do. Feel the emotions and let them roll over you. At first they are overwhelming, but as time passes, it gets easier and you feel better afterwards.

❖**Be sad.** Allow yourself to be sad and beware of the urge to "stuff" your feelings. Eventually stuffed feelings must come out. Better they come out during the grief process and not at an inappropriate time in the future.

❖**Denial is okay.** It protects you and gives you time to recuperate before you deal with your new situation. The funny thing about denial is that you don't even know you are in it, and you may let it go too long without knowing it.

•Do personal "reality checks" on your emotional and physical status.
•Ask loved ones and friends to help you evaluate where you are.
•Make sure you are in the "real world" and take care of everyday responsibilities.

❖**Honor the past.** Get out the pictures and honor what was. Don't dwell on it, but honor and remember the good things. They are an important part of who you are.

❖**Seek wise guidance.** If you need help, try support groups with other people who have gone through the same thing. Grief groups are great and are all different. Search for one that's right for you. You'll find comfort knowing others are going through the same thing and living through it. Don't be discouraged if the first support group you try isn't right for you. I went to three support groups before I found a good one. Friends and family are great, too, but it's better to find others who are at a different stage of the process than you are.

◈**Seek other survivors** or someone you admire who has gone through the same kind of loss. This person is your "grief mentor."

◈**Surround yourself with people who are "listeners," not talkers.** That could be anyone. Even strangers can be good listeners.

◈**HUGS...HUGS... HUGS!** They say you need 8 hugs a day to be emotionally healthy. Ask your 'huggee' to HOLD ON TIGHT.

◈**Pamper yourself.** Take time off for yourself. A "shrink" friend told me to get massages after my husband died… and my friend, who was lonely after her child went off to college, was told the same thing. Spend money to pamper yourself. You're no good to anyone else if you aren't good to yourself. Here are a few suggestions:

> ◈Visit a friend
> ◈Go to an art museum
> ◈Buy flowers
> ◈Sit in a sauna
> ◈Have a friend over
> ◈Rent a great movie
> ◈Start an art project
> ◈Buy an outfit
> ◈Have spa treatments … manicure, facial, massages
> ◈Do something you've always wanted to do … and never did
> ◈Go fishing

◈Instead of cleaning house, call a friend or take a walk

◈Sleep in a tent, etc. etc.

◈**Read grief books.** They help you see that your experiences are normal. I know it's hard to concentrate on reading when you hurt. If it's hard for you, read in small chunks and give yourself permission to skip around.

◈**Take care of yourself more than ever.** This is a time to get a physical, take extra vitamins, and listen to your body when it tells you something is wrong. Eat lots of fruits and vegetables, and avoid obsessive eating that may make you feel even worse physically. Drink plenty of water.

◈**Remember to breathe** deep and strong. It's amazing what good, new air can do to replenish you. Breathing helps you center and stabilize yourself when your inside meets the outside. It also helps you let go of control and relax. Breathe in through your nose and out through your mouth. The air entering your nose actually spins down into the deep part of your lungs and results in a better use of the oxygen. You are also more likely to force all the "bad air" out and let it all go. When you feel as if you are losing it, just take a deep breathe and try to relax.

◈**Exercise** helps you let go and get through the day. Your physical and mental self feel better for the stress you release (see more about stress in Chapter 5). Establish some sort of exercise routine. When you treat exercise like a regular part of the day, just like brushing your teeth, you'll find it's easy to do.

◈**Try meditation** to silence the voices and get you in touch with a larger world. Create a special, sacred, comfy place just for you and go there to enjoy the silence. This also opens up your senses and gets you in touch with yourself.

◈**Surround yourself with living things,** such as plants, goldfish, fruit, and animals. Don't isolate yourself too much. It's good to be around people, even if you aren't socializing with them. Their presence is enough to keep you alive, too.

◈**Surround yourself with lots of colors.** Go for the bright, vivid colors to spark you up a bit: yellow, orange, red, and green. Avoid black and dark blue.

◈**Go for professional help.** There is nothing wrong with professional help. Counselors are great at looking at your situation objectively and giving you support. I went to a counselor when I felt especially desperate. Just like finding the right grief group, finding the right counselor is important.

Chapter Three

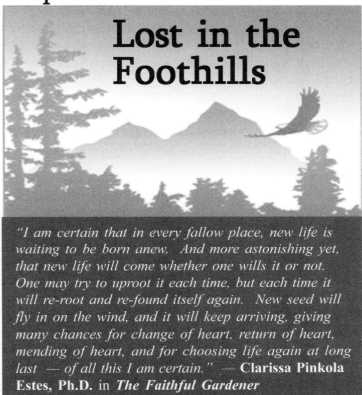

Lost in the Foothills

"I am certain that in every fallow place, new life is waiting to be born anew. And more astonishing yet, that new life will come whether one wills it or not. One may try to uproot it each time, but each time it will re-root and re-found itself again. New seed will fly in on the wind, and it will keep arriving, giving many chances for change of heart, return of heart, mending of heart, and for choosing life again at long last — of all this I am certain." — **Clarissa Pinkola Estes, Ph.D.** in *The Faithful Gardener*

Being lost in the foothills of change and transition is like being lost in the wilderness. We all have experienced the feeling of being lost. As a child, I was separated from my parents in the Museum of Science and Industry in Chicago. I remember that strong feeling of frustration, which leads to panic. Fortunately, I found someone to help.

In the wilderness, there is no help desk, police officer, or cell phone you can use to get help. Just like in the grief process, the first instinct is to deny we are lost. We lose our reference point and convince ourselves that we will find our way "just around the next bend." Reality eventually sets in and we must figure out how to save ourselves. Our situation becomes critical … even life threatening.

❖If we panic, we tend to answer the fear pumping through us with destructive behavior. We run around in circles aimlessly. That is the last thing we should do. It could cost us our lives. Physically, the adrenaline and endorphins pump fast and furiously. Our breathing becomes rapid, and we start to sweat. We deplete our resources and could run out of them faster than we realize. Mentally we become disorganized and disoriented. Our sense of reason is foggy.

❖If we calm down, get ourselves together, and form a strategy, we have a better chance of survival. To survive, we need to preserve our resources and protect ourselves outside and inside. We need to:

•Keep warm and dry, and make a shelter to protect our bodies from the elements and avoid physical depletion from the outside.

•Drink as much water as we can, and eat to protect ourselves from depletion from the inside.

•Only then can we devise a rescue plan

A universal pattern of coping with loss and adjustment to major change exists, and it is very much like what happens when we are **lost in the wilderness,** trying to find our way to safety. Fear and panic set in and we tend to run around aimlessly. Some people go to bed and stay there. Although the results of both behaviors are not necessarily life threatening, they are debilitating. **If we take care of ourselves outside and inside, we can make a plan and find ourselves again.**

Our Journey

We know we have a large mountain in our way. We can climb it, stay where we are, or wander around in the foothills. At the beginning of this journey, we are truly lost and trying to find our way. To be successful in our venture, we need to find ourselves first. **If we see who we are, we discover what we are able to become.** If I don't have a job any more, then who am I? If my kids have left home and my role as a mom is not the central part of my life any more, then who am I? If I'm not a spouse any more, then what am I?

Sometimes we must wander around lost in order to be found. We must go through the fire to ignite a spark hiding within. Nature shows the secret power buried inside us.

The Seed in the Cone

In 1997 I worked for an adventure travel company and took people on bike trips from Livingston, Montana to Jackson Hole, Wyoming. On my first trip through Yellowstone National Park, our small group of twelve started peddling through lush valleys, crisscrossed with rivers and small streams, then through full thick forests and up grueling hills onto the plateau that was Yellowstone. The landscape changed many times as we rode by hot bubbling geyser basins, waterfalls, and one thick forested area after the other. We found ourselves so immersed in nature that our moods changed as the landscape did. The joy of the bubbling river gave way to easy conversation in the great lush valleys, and then silence in the thick forest.

Nature Takes Away

Suddenly, the landscape changed dramatically as we came to an area devastated by fire. The dank, musty odor of death filled our nostrils. As our eyes adjusted to the dark, scorched earth around us, we fell silent, separating from each other to give us a private space to grieve in our own way for the trees and the animals that had perished there.

The tar black ground was scarred and sad. Leaning snags and black frazzled twigs rose from the ashes. Decaying tree trunks looked like fallen telephone poles. Tall, scorched trunks were silhouetted against the blue sky, no longer full of life, but monuments to themselves and the forest that had once been there. In their midst, a few survivors stood tall and straight, saying, "I am still here ... and I'm not giving up."

At the same time, the forest floor that had hardly seen the sun when the forest thrived was now bathed in light. Amidst death and the barren ground, short, frail, newly sprouted saplings struggled heavenward, fighting their way to life. Bright green against the black soil, those leafy and delicate sprouts resonated strength in their presence. The negativity of death and destruction gave way to the optimism of hope and new life.

Nature Gives Back

How did those saplings grow in fire-ravaged soil, in the middle of nowhere? Through the infinite resourcefulness of nature, forest fires convert the old growth into nutrient-rich fertilizer. But the fire often spares the lodge pole pine, a tall thin tree with sparse growth, and only at the very top.

Lodge pole pines produce two kinds of cones. One looks very much like the cones of other pine trees; the other is a small, sticky, nubby cone that drops to the ground and gets covered with dirt and leaves. There it waits, buried deep in the earth. It lies in dark dormancy ... and waits ... and waits ... until fire comes. In the extreme heat of a forest fire, the tiny seed explodes, releasing the hope of new life. Other cones may perish in the flames, but this sticky insignificant little cone carries the miracle of life.

New Life Begins

The saplings grow best under full sunlight and in the fertile soil following a forest fire. Spruce and fir trees flourish only under the shade of lodge pole pines, so they also start to re-populate. Wind, birds, insects, and small animals bring in seeds that before would have struggled to find a place to grow. And so the forest begins anew, reborn with species of plants and animals the land never welcomed before. Within years, the forest floor is fresh and new, bathed in abundant sunlight and rain. Life in the new forest is better and more varied than it ever was before.

So it is with us. We have a seed inside—a spirit or force that may be hidden from view until some crisis brings it to the fore, and then we become fresh and new. The devastation of major loss or change brings with it new opportunities to turn ourselves in another direction, to shed our old skin, and to re-build who we are. As with the forest, our loss opens up more space to welcome new dreams, and with those dreams come new actions, relationships, growth, and creativity.

But we must let the land be fallow so the soil can rest, and we must have patience. For the sapling, the fire creates a fertile environment, nature gives it the essential gifts of light and water, and, when the time is right, with a final push, the courageous little tree bursts through the soil. Like the sapling, we push, we grow, we struggle, and we become a tree, straight and tall.

With fire and loss comes the knowledge that life constantly renews itself. No matter how many times fire ravages the land, no matter how many times we are beaten down, the indomitable spirit of new growth is there … waiting to spring to life again.

Pharmaceutical company Johnson & Johnson certainly sprang to new life after fire tested it in 1982. That year, Tylenol capsules laced with cyanide caused the deaths of seven people. As soon as the link was made between the capsules and the deaths, Johnson & Johnson spread the word quickly on a vast scale to prevent further deaths. Serving their mission statement that puts the customer first, they contacted the media, told consumers to steer clear of Tylenol capsules, and instituted a massive recall. The recall of 31 million bottles of Tylenol cost the company $125 million.

With those losses behind them, they raced to re-launch Tylenol in new tamper- proof packaging. Within one year, the sales of Tylenol returned to where they had been before the crisis. Why? They had gained the people's respect and trust as they supported the families of the seven victims. They served the public interest during tough times and were upfront and honest about what the company did and didn't know. They focused on protecting the public's safety at all costs, not on the impact of negative news. They did the right thing! They sprang to life again.

But how can we look at the aftermath of destruction as devastating as the World Trade Center attack and see the seed in the cone? That amazing fire and destruction shook the foundation of our lives and yet some good things came out of it that may, in the end, make us better Americans and better people in the world community.

For example, we have learned to appreciate our freedom, our families, and our country. We have learned to be aware of other cultures and religions that we knew nothing about before. We have learned to look with fresh eyes at the way other people are treated. We have learned to analyze what our own responsibilities are to others. We have learned that we, as a people, had taken much for granted and not appreciated. Most important, we have learned to read the papers regularly and understand more about our own political situation and our policies.

So, just as the forest needs to be stripped of overgrown and unhealthy trees in order to stay young and vital, perhaps the 9-11 destruction provides us with a chance for rebirth of a more vital nation.

Finding Ourselves

Who Are We?

Climbing the mountain in our way is not only about overcoming the situation in our path; **it's also about finding ourselves** and redefining ourselves in a new life. Finding our confidence and self-esteem is part of the vision we have for our new self.

Who you were, you are no longer. That's what change does. However, you still carry the sources of who you are, where you came from, and what you experienced in the past. We are born with genetic traits that will always be with us, including what we look like, our main personality traits, what family we grew up in, where we lived, contacts we've made, and experiences we've had over the years. These are all part of who we are.

Our roles also define us, including our job, our martial status, our age, our sexual orientation, our ethnic background, our physical and mental gifts or handicaps, and even our birthplace. In our society, we are also defined by the possessions we have, the car we drive, the kind of house we live in, the amount of money we have earned, who reports to us at work, and who we work with. The list is endless. But realize this: **the role definitions, and the judgments society makes based on these roles are not really who we are.**

My Husband the Tree

Two years after Tom died, I went on a trekking expedition to the base camp of Mt. Everest. Wonderful Sherpa porters accompanied and supported the expedition group. The Sherpas were kind and gentle people, small in stature but large in heart, with olive skin and beautiful red cheeks. They had an amazingly peaceful look in their eyes and always smiled. As Buddhists, they measured their success not by the possessions they had, but by the kindness they showed in serving others.

As the Sherpas set up camp the first night, I couldn't help but notice the stares I got. I saw them whisper and turn their backs, as if they were trying to stifle a big secret. At first I thought they were just having fun, laughing about my white blonde hair, but later, I found out the real reason.

In their culture, a widow is the very bottom of the caste system and bad luck. The Sherpas worried about having a widow as part of the group and were certain that bad luck would follow us. All along the way up to the base camp, they threw handfuls of rice to offset the bad luck I brought. But they had a solution. If I were married, I would be acceptable. So in a grove of olive trees, and under a particularly beautiful one, I was married ...to a tree. (Oh, if we could all be married to such a strong, steadfast, and beautiful spouse, unconditional and non-judgmental.)

I was defined as the bottom of the bottom in the caste system ... not by who I was, but by how their society perceived me.

Who We Really Are

Our lives are like a patchwork quilt, made up of many pieces. All the pieces are different colors and shapes, some colorful and bright, while others are dull and lifeless. Some pieces are large and some quite small. But each piece is necessary to make the whole. All are part of who we are: experiences, people we have been in contact with, important events, how we grew up, and our family life. We need all of them to make the whole. When new pieces are added to what's already there, they adjust to fit. **The quilt is so much richer and more beautiful**

for the variety we put in. Most important, the quilt is a work in progress, not completed until we die.

Who Are We Now?

With loss and change, our definition of who we are changes, as does our self-worth. We think of ourselves as we used to be, using the definitions from society. **When things change, those self-definitions we have used over the years no longer fit.** For example, I went from a wife, suburban homemaker, and small business owner to a widow, city dweller, apartment renter, job searcher, and lonely person all in a split-second.

I remember my divorced friend telling me how her "wandering" husband, who left her for another woman, destroyed her confidence. I can't imagine what that kind of rejection must feel like, to say nothing of the loss of self-esteem and confidence. She was amazed to find out that as a widow I also felt a lack of self-confidence. No matter who we are, **the life we lead and our partnerships define us.** When it's gone, we are like a bird with one wing, and it is very hard to fly.

Having my own small business and running it efficiently out of my house was something I was very proud of. Unfortunately, I had to quit my business when my life changed, because I could no longer make it work financially with three boys in college and a big mortgage. That part of my life was over and I needed to join the workforce with skills that would not transfer to the available job market. My self-definition had to change, and how I felt about myself went right down the tubes with it.

If you've lost a job, you've lost the position that defined you, the money you made that allowed you to pay your bills (hopefully!), the responsibilities you had, and the relationships with your colleagues.

Who are you now? Your trip up the mountain helps you to find that out, and you **may** even find something better than what you had before.

> *"The worst past of losing a job is losing self-esteem."*
> **Richard Boles**, author of *What Color is Your Parachute?*

The truth is, we may not have changed at all. Deep down inside, we are still basically the same, but we must change to accommodate a new life. **Ending the old us and beginning the new is what transition is all about.** We have lost self-esteem because we no longer know what direction we are going. We don't know if we're capable of surviving. We don't even know if we are lovable anymore! The good news is that self-esteem returns with time and experience. When we comfortably walk a new road, our selves are reborn. We come back new and strong, just like the seed in the cone.

Going it Alone

It's amazing how the people around us react when we go through major change. For fear of not saying "the right thing," they say nothing at all. For fear of facing their own pain, they don't want to see you face-to-face. For fear of letting you know how sorry they feel for you, they stay away so they won't have to talk to you about your situation. Well-meaning people—family, co-workers, bosses, friends, and other acquaintances—want to help, but they just don't know how ... so **they stay away** and we feel rejected and alone.

Many well-meaning people **give you advice** about how to "get over it" based on their own experiences. They don't like the disturbance in the status quo. In truth, no one likes this grief period, so we all struggle for the quick fix. Advice is meant to minimize or fix the problem so it will go away.

My brother said to me, "I know just how you feel. I was divorced twice. And then I was alone." Divorce devastated for him, I'm sure, but his situation was different than mine. He can't know how I feel. He's not me. Others will say, "Just stay busy all the time, and it will pass." Good idea, but it's not that easy. The advice we get from others is well-meaning, but reflects perceptions that may not hold true for us.

Having a loving family around and friends who can speak and love honestly and unconditionally is a real gift. Not everyone has that gift. The funny thing is, **if you don't have family and friends around, people often "drop" into your life to help you.** I don't know why that happens ... it just does! Many strangers I met along the way took my hand and led me.

The one thing we know about transition is this: We can't ignore the mountain. We have a hole in our heart, and our drive is to fill it in our own way. We must find our own way. In the process, we find ourselves.

Finding Authenticity

We all have a basic desire to please others and be loved and appreciated for who we are. This is deeply rooted in how we grew up, starting with parents and teachers, to friends and peers. As adults, we try to teach our children a standard of behavior based on what we felt was right and compatible with our values and style of living. **We hope our children do not grow up to be us, but that they use what we teach them to become who they were meant to be.**

However, sometimes we must resort to brainwashing!

As teenagers, my boys thought I was the stupidest person they had ever known (aren't we all?). So I brainwashed them into thinking I was brilliant. Every afternoon after school, we watched the TV game show *Jeopardy*, which involved contestants answering questions, with the winner getting the most right. I won *every single time!* My sons thought I was "really smart." At my oldest son's wedding I confessed the root of my brilliance: every day I got the answers from my mom who saw the program on TV several hours earlier in Florida! For that brief period in my children's lives, I was incredibly smart. So much for authenticity!

The challenge is to find our authentic self … the seed in our cone, where our passion is, what makes us tick, what we value, who we want to associate with, what we do to be happy and fulfilled. With this comes the re-emergence of our self-esteem and self-confidence. Sometimes it takes the fire of change to discover that real, tough, core person hidden inside.

How do we find the authentic self to be strong and confident? **We do it by:**

- ❖ journaling, as it helps you unearth the real you;
- ❖ asking questions and learning as much as you can;
- ❖ getting help when you need it;
- ❖ reading and studying;
- ❖ soul searching;

◈   saying affirmations to support yourself;

◈   finding your spiritual base; and

◈   **choosing to climb that mountain!** When you do, you get stronger and stronger with every step, and learn about yourself along the way.

Choosing to Climb

Choosing to climb is choosing life and moving on. It sounds simplistic, I know! It's frightening and painful to face that journey into the unknown, especially when you would love to hold on and stay where you are. But climbing your mountain doesn't mean you're giving up the life you had before. Instead you take it with you and use it as building blocks for the new person you are becoming.

Climbing the mountain will:

◈   teach you who you are;

◈   help you get your feet on the ground;

◈   show you what's ahead for you;

◈   catapult you in to new life;

◈   teach you new skills;

◈   help you honor the past;

◈   reorient you;

◈   open up possibilities;

◈   help you get more comfortable trying new things;

◈   get you in touch with the spiritual;

◈   get you in touch with others;

◈   show you how to trust the process;

◈   open yourself up to synchronicity;

◈   hone your climbing skills.

Okay, you're going to climb! You have nowhere to go but up and a clean slate to start with. You have nothing to lose. The first step of your new life starts right now. It's time to prepare for survival.

Survival Tips

◆Just be. Live in the moment and grab the good ones when they come. You will learn to appreciate them more than you ever did. You will also find that when you concentrate on those positive moments, they will eventually overshadow the negative ones.

◆Slow down. If you feel panic setting in, try to calm yourself down, sit back, and relax or distract yourself by doing something you enjoy. The feeling of being lost, alone, and out of control will pass with time.

◆Schedule yourself. I know it doesn't sound as if it goes with **just be**, but it does. If you have a schedule, you can space out the ugly parts of your life. Some people in transition mentally fly around all over the place and need to schedule a little so they can go on living, especially now, when they are more scattered than usual. A schedule will help you get out of bed, get things done, and help reduce the chaos.

◆No need to be a perfectionist. If you're sick of housework, chores, or tedious stuff, then don't do those things for a while. It's okay if your surroundings aren't perfect. I would love to tell you to forget the painful things such as the bills, but you simply must do some things. If you can't face the tough tasks, ask someone to help you. People love to help.

◆Affirmations are a great way to boost your self-worth. Say good things about yourself in the present tense, such as, "I'm really efficient. I can do anything I put my mind to," or "I'm fine on my own. The world is full of possibilities for me." Write them down and stick them on your mirror. Say them to yourself over and over. What you say becomes reality.

◆Find your comfort things. My friends bought me a full-length body pillow I affectionately named Robert Redford. He wore a hat and tie and stretched the whole length of the bed. My foot rested against him when I was asleep. He helped me feel less alone.

My friend, who went through a serious bout with cancer, received a bear from one of her friends. The bear sat with her through all of her treatments and recuperation. When she was cancer free, she passed the bear on to another friend, Barbara, when her husband died. She has it now and will pass it on when she is better.

◈**Journal.** Journaling does wonders in helping you clean out your head and work through your feelings and concerns. To get the most from journaling, follow these guidelines:

    ◈Pick the best time of day for you. Be flexible. Some days are easier than others. Do it every day.

    ◈Decide how long you will write.

    ◈Don't stop once you start.

    ◈Don't judge yourself; just do it.

    ◈Don't read what you write.

    ◈Free flow it; write anything, even the weather if that's all you can think of. Just don't stop.

The amazing thing about journaling is that after the first ten minutes or two pages, you start writing all sorts of profound things that you never knew you had in you ... and you really can work things out.

◈**Allow yourself to do dumb things.** You *will* do things that are out of character. Somebody told me I would, and I didn't believe them. I did them anyway. If you find yourself behaving this way, just make sure not to hurt yourself or other people in the process.

◈**Watch the rebound.** If you've lost a loved one, watch the rebound. We are all searching for love. I was lonely but grateful that I didn't meet someone when I was vulnerable and needy. You can get yourself in trouble by falling for the wrong person out of loneliness. Substituting one strong emotion for another may just postpone the grief you need to experience and learn from. If you have lost a job, be careful not to "jump" at the first one that comes along, especially if it isn't right for you.

Part II
Reviving

"Up to a point, a man's life is shaped by environment, heredity, and movements and changes in the world around him. Then there comes a time when it is within his grasp to shape the clay of this life into the sort of thing he wishes to be. .... Everyone has it within his power to say: THIS is who I am today, THAT I will be tomorrow."

—Louis L'Amour

Chapter Four

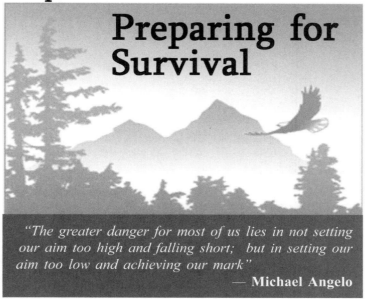

Preparing for Survival

"The greater danger for most of us lies in not setting our aim too high and falling short; but in setting our aim too low and achieving our mark"
— **Michael Angelo**

Mountain climbing is tedious work and requires mental and physical preparation. Investing the time, resources, and energy to get ready will make the unforeseen challenges easier to scale. Doubting your abilities and questioning your persistence during this climb are all part of the process. At times, you will feel exhausted and will have to push yourself to move on. Preparation is the key to rising above those times and having a successful climb. The elements of preparation are:

◈**Educating yourself** on the journey you have chosen assures that you at least have some idea where you're going and how you'll get there. If you know about the potential roadblocks you may encounter, you will be better prepared to deal with them.

◈**Mental preparation** assures that you are mentally self-assured and confident that you will succeed. When you doubt yourself and want to quit along the way, mental preparation helps you get through it.

◈**Physical preparation** and training are necessary to make sure you succeed when the going gets tough. The path will be difficult at times for sure. If you're in top physical shape, you'll get through the rigors of the climb and the challenges along the way.

Identifying where you want to go, analyzing how you will get there, and making sure you are prepared to achieve success are the keys to survival.
Being stuck between the old and new life gives us the opportunity to reinvent ourselves and find a new path. Educating ourselves allows us to find a new road map. The challenges we face during transition and major change require us to be prepared. The emotional challenges add difficulty to the process, but with time and the experience of the climb, we can make progress. Preparation makes us lighter on our feet, better at making decisions, and may help us keep the obstacles in perspective.

After Tom died, I had no husband, no home, and no financial means. I had to quickly figure out what I needed, what my current skills were, and what I could learn fast.

At the time, I had a successful wood crafting business that provided a great secondary income. Unfortunately, it was not enough to support me and my three boys in college. So I decided to get a job that would provide more income and medical benefits. I needed a job in a large company.

It took me three weeks to learn word processing. I struggled through books, phone calls with experienced people, and hours of practice. Then I went to a temporary employment agency. As I drove to the office, I heard a song on the radio that brought me to tears. I arrived at my interview with red swollen eyes. I looked in the rear view mirror and said to myself, "Okay. This is your only chance. You go out there and smile and do your best."

The typing test was the first surprise. Like a woman possessed, I typed twice as fast as ever before with no mistakes. I took the computer skills test on a program I had never seen before…and I passed. All my preparation paid off.

The Vision Ahead

Knowing where you are going is not easy. When change happens, our old vision takes a detour. What we wanted and are able to achieve are no longer possible. In the transition period we redefine ourselves and also what we want out of life. Major change alters our view of the world and profoundly affects who we are.

At the beginning we have no idea who we are, where we are, and where we are going. At this time, it's okay to think in terms of making it day-to-day… moment by moment. During the darkest times, I felt that living through the pain of each day was enough of a vision. I pictured myself not feeling it and living anyway. I knew happiness was beyond my reach, so just existing was an accomplishment. This short-term vision eventually leads to higher ones in the future.

Determining *your* higher vision means letting go of the critics (you and other people) who stop you from thinking big. I'm great at telling myself something is too hard for me, or that I won't like something long before I even try it. Very often, we are own worst critic.

Sometimes other people look at what you envision for yourself and say, **"Oh, that can't be done,"** or **"No way. That's already been tried and it won't work. You will fail,"** or **"It's just too hard … you're a fool if you try."** You don't need to take the road others have taken. You don't need to listen to the skeptics who have doubts about everything. Take the road less traveled—the road that has never been tried or the road that doesn't even exist. You may have to work a little harder, struggle a little more, but you will be following your own vision. This is a perfect time to reinvent yourself.

Your vision is your greatest possibility … your ultimate dream. Your vision is where your passion is, and your passion is where your energy is. It gives your life meaning. It's compatible with your beliefs. Your passion makes your blood flow a little faster and makes you pop out of a chair when you think about it. It makes you wake up in the morning and sing in the shower. Imagine what your life would be like if you could live this passion every moment of every day.

"Reach high, for the stars lie hidden in your soul.
Dream deep, for every dream precedes the goal."
— **Pamela Starr**

Create your vision with enough space so you can change and alter it when necessary. Being too tied to a vision and dream means you will not have enough space for the unforeseen to enter, for the path to change, or for a new opportunity to present itself. Realize that your path will go the course it is meant to go. Having space and being open to *all* possibilities along the way helps you find what you *really* envisioned for yourself all along.

Sometimes the path is the goal. For example, the remarkable woman known as the Peace Pilgrim walked from town to town all over the United States to spread her message of peace. She walked for 28 years, from 1953-1981. In the first eleven years, she walked over 25,000 miles, and then she stopped counting. She carried with her only the bare necessities: a toothbrush, a comb, a pen and paper, and the fliers containing her message of peace. She said the purpose of her pilgrimage was twofold: (1) to connect with the people personally and through media to spread her message of non-violence, and (2) to create prayer discipline. For the Peace Pilgrim, her path was her goal. She had no specific goals in mind. She anticipated no outcomes. She simply lived by her convictions and let her passion lead the way.

Sometimes you will not be able to get what you want. Some people never get what they strive for, no matter what they do. If that's the case, stay awake and make short-term goals that make life livable: find alternative sources of happiness, try to find the good in what you do, and look beyond it. Open yourself up to new possibilities for fulfillment.

During transition, we are all floundering and a little lost, **so it's hard to know what we really want for ourselves.** All we want is what we had before, and that isn't possible. We can't go back. I knew I needed to find myself again, and I had no idea how. As I thought of what really *excited* me and gave me warm fuzzy feelings, I started to find my passion. I went from envisioning myself sitting at a desk doing paperwork to writing a book and speaking to groups of people. One sounded incredibly dull, and the other pumped me up.

Passion To Vision to Action

How do you find your passion?
Think of it this way:

◈**What do you love to do?** Think about what you loved to do as a child. Some of those things are still true and part of your nature. Think about how you would love to spend your ideal day. What do you need to do before you get too old to do it? What will you regret if you don't do it?

◈**With whom do you like to associate?** What kind of people spark your energy and make you feel great? For example, some people are energized by athletic people, some by intellectual people. Some people feel great being around logical left-brained people, and some like creative right-brained ones. Some people like to surround themselves with lots of family. Your passion revolves around the company you keep. They are your emotional and intellectual support.

◈**What skills do you have and what do you love to learn?** I had a client who said, "I don't have any special skills." **YES YOU DO!** We all have something we're good at ... even if it's not obvious. Consider this:

- Are you good at crunching numbers?
- Do you love computers and analyzing things?
- Do you love to read?
- Are you a sports enthusiast?
- Are you great with animals?
- Are you a good listener?
- Are you a good caretaker?

◈**What is your personality like?** Are you:
- Introverted or extroverted (energized by being alone or energized by being with others)?
- Organized or disorganized?

- Creative or logical?
- A team player or a solitary worker?
- Fast-paced or slow-paced?

◈ **What do you value the most?**

- Do you value family and taking care of other people?
- Do you thirst for learning and value books, analyzing what's in them?
- Do you love power and money? Do you have a desire to acquire?
- Are you creative? Do you love the arts?
- Are you athletic? Do you value physical activity and good health?
- Are you a "cause person," striving to make a difference by fighting for a cause you are passionate about?

Put all these things together and you will find your passion. You'll soon discover that your passion has been a part of you your entire life. **You don't choose your passion; your passion chooses you at birth.** Finding your passion is about following your instincts.

Living with the energy and focus born of passion makes your life come alive. That energy will carry you through the tough times. It cuts through fear and exhaustion and allows you to keep going. Loving what you do gives your life meaning and purpose.

Instinct Is The Passion From Your Heart

During grief and transition, your **instincts peak.** The need to survive awakens your emotions in preparation for fight or flight. Now is when you need to search for inner guidance from your instincts. It tells you where your passion is.

Follow what you know about yourself. Your heart will tell you what is right and wrong for you. Listen for that still, small voice inside driving you forward, as it will show you the direction to go. Your vision is not necessarily a destination, but a path; it's a guide that leads you where you are supposed to go.

The hardest part is listening to that voice inside and finding the courage to follow it.

Imagination Gives Your Passion Form

Your mind translates those instincts into a vision of what is possible and what fits for you. Your vision may not be a destination but will guide you in the right direction. When you actually imagine it, see it, and hear it, you understand how you COULD live.

Instinct ⟶ **Imagination** ⟶ **Vision**
Feel it ⟶ **See and hear it** ⟶ **It becomes reality**

Just imagine the possibilities ahead, given who you are, what you like, what you value, and all the skills you have. Get it in your head, see it, and feel it into reality. Know where you are going, then turn this vision into action.

Vision to Action

Your vision is nothing until you put it into action. If you do not put your vision into action with concrete goals or plans, then you'll get nowhere.

Before climbing a mountain, I visualize myself standing on the top. My arms are outstretched and I'm looking out over all the peaks below me. I feel energized. I breathe deeply and take in all the beauty before me. Somehow it becomes a part of me, and I become part of a presence larger than myself. I'm connected to the whole world.

As I start up the mountain, my vision is to get over the next hill, to make it to the end of the day, to notice what nature is showing me along the way, and to make it to the next water break. Grand visions set far in the future are only made possible by the small goals set along the way. One by one, they lead me where I want to go.

Saying, "Okay, I know what I want and how I will get there" seems a little scary, especially after a major change. But setting a plan is the starting point in going towards the vision. And remember that it's adjustable as you go.

Once you know it and speak it, support seems to "show up." You tell the universe and everyone in it that this will be, and it is. Your intention opens you up to the support and encouragement of others. Sharing with the world around you reinforces your convictions, even to yourself.

After Tom died, I lived in Illinois. I felt out of place there and knew it wasn't right. So I thought about my passion, about what I loved to do, who I loved to be with, and my skills, personality, and values. I thought about what my instincts were telling me. When I could envision my passion for myself, I spoke it and drew a picture of it.

I always wanted to live in the mountains. I had mountain climbed all my life, and they became a part of who I was. This was where my spirit came alive. So I envisioned a little log cabin on top of a mountain, surrounded by a beautiful forest and a bubbling river. In my cabin, I envisioned a fireplace with a small rug in front of it and a cozy fire burning in the fireplace. In my vision I'm sitting in my comfy chair, listening to the crackling of the fire, and am filled by the fresh smell of pine surrounding me. I'm awakened from my reverie when my Golden Retriever sighs and shifts position.

Deep down inside, I knew this vision could never be mine. I lived in Chicago and had no financial means to attain it or the heart to seek it out. Tom and I had acquired a parcel of land on top of a mountain just outside Steamboat Springs, Colorado. It was sitting there empty since the day before he died. That very day, we dug the foundation of our cabin on top of the mountain. That dream died with him.

The land was one of those emotional ties I had with Tom's memory that I just couldn't part with. Then one day, I got a call from a real estate broker telling me that a family was interested in purchasing the land. In order to avoid taxes, I had to use the proceeds to buy something within 90 days.

Today, I do have a small log home *near* the top of a mountain. I have a bubbling stream nearby and I always keep a fire crackling in the fireplace. I'm grateful for the nudge I was given by unseen forces that heard me speak my vision.

Timing is Everything

If you have experienced the loss of a loved one and are deep into the grief process, time is a soft pillow for you to sink yourself into and wallow in. When you are ready to emerge from that place, time becomes a friend to run with. That time of marinating your feelings and thoughts gives way to the action born of pain and self-discovery. Every second seems to count.

If you have lost a job, health and clear thoughts come after you take time to process the loss in your head. You need to get on with life, but moving too fast can lead you on a detour.

In our culture, which is ruled by technology, addicted to speed, and based on instant gratification, time has a different meaning. We think that those who don't keep up fall behind forever. Time is not to be squandered but used efficiently. At times of uncertainty, however, time is a gift because it sends us off in another direction. It puts a halt to the direction we are going, stops us, and sends us off again. It gives us the opportunity to look at time again and use it for processing and clarifying.

Time is both a gift and a curse. When you are in pain, time seems to go slowly, and as things get better, it rushes along. Regardless, time always passes. So honor it, because when it's gone, it's gone forever.

"Half our life is spent trying to find something to do with the time we have rushed through life trying to save."
— **Will Rogers**

Are You Ready?

Rushing into an aggressive plan before you're emotionally ready could leave you even more emotionally devastated. Granted, people often want to get the grief and transition part over with so they can move on and be normal again. But you must stabilize before making a major move. Figuring out your vision takes some time, and rushing into goals you aren't ready for could lead to a setback.

For example, I really wanted that log cabin in Steamboat Springs, so three months after Tom died, I rushed there to see if I could figure out a way to do it. I even interviewed a Chicago-person who had moved there to get his opinion on how I could do it. He told me that it's hard to make it there financially, and that single people are looked down on. I listened to him and was emotionally devastated. Driving away from that meeting, I did a 360-degree spinout in the snow on the highway and hit a tree, disabling my car. I had to carry two suitcases down the highway in the snow to get back to town, and I cried all the way to Chicago. I was nowhere near ready for any of this. I was rushing too fast, too soon.

Are Your Goals Reachable?

The one thing you don't want to do is set yourself up for failure before you even start. While you do want to stretch yourself and your goals, you also need to know your own personal limits.

When I climbed to the base camp of Mt. Everest at age 52, I was certain that I could not reach the peak. I wasn't physically fit or experienced enough. Attempting it would have meant my own failure and could have jeopardized other people, too. So the base camp was my limit … and that was reachable.

Realize that you can't control everything. You can't control unforeseen problems that come, the people who throw you a curve, or acts of God or Mother Nature. You can't control the social environment or what the economy does. But your goals are reachable if you are aware of those things you *can* control.

So, ask yourself the following:

◈ Given what I know, can I be prepared enough to succeed, to learn what I need to learn, to be mentally ready to face the challenges, and emotionally ready to move on?

◈ Are the goals congruent with who I am, what I've done in the past, what lifestyle I'm comfortable with, and what I want to do?

◈ Am I flexible enough to adjust as I go along *just in case* the uncontrollables get in my way?

Total Preparation

When climbing a mountain, real or metaphorical, supporting yourself by being prepared makes the journey much easier. Rushing into action without the proper preparation is asking for failure. If I try to climb a mountain without getting myself in top physical condition first, I will fail and cause others in my group fail, too. If I'm not mentally ready, not totally committed, have a negative attitude, or am emotionally fragile, I assure failure for all of us. If I don't surround myself with people who are also prepared, who are supportive, and who are team players, then we will all fail.

Physical Preparation

Taking care of yourself physically is the key to surviving any climb. During any challenging situation, those with a lower level of physical fitness struggle more along the way. Similarly, getting through the grief process or a transitional stage is harder when you are physically taxed. Being in top physical condition makes you feel better and think clearer. Here's how you can be in top physical condition:

◈**Exercising** regularly keeps the blood flowing, engages the endorphins, and keeps the mind sharp.

◈**Stretching** keeps the muscles healthy and the body relaxed and balanced.

◈**Eating right** keeps the furnace stoked and the mind and body in tune.

◈**Taking vitamins** keeps the inside balanced just right.

◈**Having a check up** keeps you on track.

◈**Looking your best** keeps your self-image compatible with how you now feel.

Intellectual Preparation

If you are climbing a mountain you must:
◈Check the route;
◈Learn about the terrain;
◈Find out about the animals that live there;
◈Analyze the safety issues you may encounter;
◈Learn about the potential obstacles you may find;
◈Find out what food and equipment you need to take.

You simply must know everything you can if you are to succeed.

The same is true during a time of transition. You need to know everything about your situation and the new environment in which you are living. In a business situation, you must know about your business, the competition, the economy, and the people you work with. Read everything you can get your hands on, study, talk to experts, and practice the skills you need. When climbing your mountain, you need to be prepared to handle the unknown roadblocks when they come. During this time you learn where you fit in, what the possibilities are, and how you can move on from here.

My financial situation after Tom died was grim. I had a little life insurance, but surely not enough to live on for very long. I couldn't spend the insurance money on everyday living expenses. I decided to invest the money – something I didn't know anything about. I had to prepare for the financial mountain in my path.

I took an investment class at Northwestern University. I didn't like getting advice from people without a clue what they were talking about. The class was my way of taking back control of my life. So my mission was to learn everything I could about investing.

Everyone in the class was young and smart, except for Susie, the person sitting next to me. Susie was about my age. Looking at Susie was like looking in the mirror: she had short blond hair and wore hiking boots and a sports watch. Both of us were clueless about the world of finance.

Before the professor handed out the first assignment, she asked, "How many people in this class have not had corporate finance?" Susie and I were the only ones to raise our hands. The professor then handed out two large packets, which were our assignments. Packet A called for doing a personal tax return; packet B, a corporate tax return. Susie and I looked at each other and burst out laughing. We continued laughing all the way to my apartment, where we faxed both packets to the tax department of the local bank.

And that's the way we got through the class… we laughed a lot, faxed the painfully hard assignments to various experts we knew, did the assignments together, and then called the experts for explanation. Both of us got A's in the class as well as the information we needed at the time. That class was a necessary survival tool for me.

Mental Preparation

Mental preparation means adopting the *adventure attitude* (more on this in chapter 6 – The Adventure Attitude). It's about training yourself to view life positively and setting yourself up for success. It's about having fun in your life again, and opening up your creativity. It's about looking at your vision and putting all your energy behind it.

Emotional Preparation

A major part of the preparation is setting up your support group. Let your dreams be known to those who will support you unconditionally – those who believe in you, who encourage you, and who give you advice when obstacles get in your path. This support group is a key to your success (see chapter 10… throwing the rope).

Survival Tips

◈ **Get up and move in the morning.**
Avoid the pitfall of sleeping too much, as it will cause you to become lethargic. Lethargy feeds on itself and before you know it, you'll spiral into total inactivity. To be healthy and fit, the body needs rest, but it also needs to move and function.

◈ **Have a structure.** In your job or in your old life, you had a routine/structure that you were accustomed to. Set up an interim structure to replace the old patterns and allow room for adjustment with some free time. This helps you get up in the morning, get moving, *and* makes you think more creatively.

◈ **Allow time to marinate.** Just like a fine tea, you need time to steep. If you have lost a job, give yourself three to four weeks to steep: reassess, analyze, and take care of yourself. Get your personal head together before you get into the job search mode. Caution: This only works for a short time and can easily turn into procrastination.

◈ **Make a list of 50 things you enjoy doing.** Write them down quickly, without thinking, to flush out your real desires. If you think too much, you tend to judge the items as you write them, and that stops you from finding your real passion. I found the first 25 were easy to write and the last 25 were harder. When done, though, you see a pattern and repetition to your list. Your passion will soon be apparent.

◈ **Determine what you're good at.** Think of skills you were born with and those you have developed over the years. Think of hard skills and personality strengths you have developed. Are they compatible with what you want to do?

◈ **Determine what you need to do.** What would you do if you only had six months to live?

•Who would you want to spend time with?

- What job would you do?
- Where would you live?
- If money were no object, what would you do for a living?

◈ **Determine your personality traits.** Is what you want compatible with the kind of person you are? Are you energized by being alone or with others? Do you like to be in control, or are you happy following? Are you always on the go, or do you like a slower pace?

◈ **Define your core values.** Think about what really matters to you. What do you value? Are you living congruently with those values? Define them, and then prioritize them and make sure your vision is on target.

◈ **Tweak your passion.** Think of all the creative ways you can tweak your passion and turn it into a life's work or a new lifestyle. You're just dreaming now, but this kind of creative thinking opens new doors of possibility for you.

◈ **Define your goals.** What do you need to do to live your passion? Think of the steps you can take that will drive you in the right direction. Write down monthly goals, weekly goals, and daily goals. Go from there to immediate goals.

◈ **Connect your goals to rewards.** Think of each goal individually and connect it to the rewards or satisfaction you will get by achieving that goal. Will it be fun to complete? Will you feel more secure if you do it? Will you feel power, excitement, or pleasure? Write down each one. Once you think in terms of rewards, your goals will be much easier to strive for.

◈ **Learn all you can.** Study, study, study. Take classes to open up possibilities, but don't overburden yourself. Pressure on top of pressure can turn into blow-up. When you grieve, you will notice that it is hard to concentrate. So, if you can, take something enjoyable and easy to get into the study/learning mode little by little. You'll find it can be fun.

◈**Make a serious exercise schedule.** Start out slow. Make sure your schedule is doable and not too hard or too long. You will find working out easier every day, and it will become a routine before you know it. Exercise does wonders for your physical and emotional well-being.

Chapter Five

Lightening Your Pack

"The ability to simplify means to eliminate the unnecessary so that the necessary may speak."
— **Hans Hoffman**

Many times, I have forgotten how important it is to take a light pack when climbing a mountain, and I have suffered for it. When you carry a pack that is too heavy, you experience consequences that make travel difficult, such as:

◆ You travel slowly.

◆ It's hard to move freely.

◆ You may not be able to negotiate obstacles in your way.

◆ It's painful.

◆ You may burn out.

◆ You may not be strong enough to make it.

◆ It's hard to see where you are.

◆ You can't communicate with others.

◆ You may become a burden to your whole group.

◆ You focus on the struggle.

◆ You don't appreciate the beauty around you.

The Heavy Pack

Climbing in the Wind River Range in Wyoming in 1982, we all knew what we could carry and what equipment we needed to bring. One person decided that he was also going to carry his camera tripod, an extra medical kit, an inflatable pillow, and some extra clothes, which made his pack the heaviest one of all. We were all afraid that his burden would be too great and that he would have a hard time keeping up. We were also fearful that his heavy pack could lead to injury. But, you can't *make* people do what *you* want them to do, so he forged ahead anyway. As if to prove a point, he held his spot at the front of the line and did just fine ... *until* he slipped and fell and landed on his ice ax. He broke a few ribs and couldn't bear the weight of his backpack. We had no choice but to divvy up his extra weight amongst the rest of us. This was a problem because it meant we were *all* carrying too much weight.

The moral: Extra baggage not only stops you from moving freely, but it can also become a burden those around you have to carry.

Often, grief and change feel a lot like carrying a heavy pack. Heavy emotions make it hard to function. Other people's burdens, obligations, and personal clutter add to the weight. What extra baggage are we already carrying?

◈ **Relationships** – Relationships can sap us and drain away our energy. We all know people who lean on us and hold us down, adding to the emotional pressure. Sometimes these people unload their personal problems on us every time we see them. We also know nay-sayers: people who say, "You can't do that," "You shouldn't try that," or "That's a stupid idea." All this extra baggage makes travel difficult.

◈ **Stuff** – Think about the piles of stuff that just sit there – the clutter in the closet, and the material things that accumulate. Several months after Tom died, I had to move from my five-bedroom house into a studio apartment for financial reasons. I had no choice but to have a massive garage sale, and I sold everything except the most meaningful family possessions. The most painful decision I had to make was to give up my two Golden Retrievers. As painful as it was, I eventually found a wonderful family to take them. Afterwards I felt light and unencumbered. I had no meaningless possessions, no big cleaning projects, no lawn to cut, and no security issues. I also released a huge financial burden that weighed me down. I could travel light!

◈**Obligations** – Do you ever find yourself saying "Yes" to things you're sorry about later? I do. For whatever reason, I fill my calendar with way too many things, and then feel the burden of the heavy pack. Grief and change give us the perfect excuse to get rid of all those, too. Letting go of commitments, obligations, and frills gives us energy because we are getting rid of those things that drain us regularly. Giving ourselves permission to take care of our own business and doing what needs to be done to survive results in carrying a lighter pack.

◈**The Past** – What about all those things from the past that hold us down? Those things that happened in the past that we are sorry for? The regrets we would like to redo, but can't? The things that happened to us that we are angry about? The good and bad experiences we carry out of the past hang around our necks and add weight to our pack. Getting out from the burden of the past means letting go and forgiving those who have wronged us, as well as letting go and forgiving ourselves. Only then can we move on unencumbered.

When I ride a bike, I wear a helmet with a small mirror attached to it so I can see what's behind me. I can protect myself by getting out of the way if I need to. But as I look in this mirror, I must remember:

◈The image is magnified, so the object appears much larger than it is. I remember the scene in *Jurassic Park* when a group fleeing a T-Rex glanced in the rear view mirror and saw the large dinosaur bearing down on them. The camera slowly panned on the rear view mirror and to the words: "Objects in the mirror are closer than they appear." The same is true in life. Sometimes the monsters in your past mesmerize you and hold you back. They loom larger than they really are.

◆ The image is distorted. As such, I don't see the dinosaur looming down on me as it really is. It is an inaccurate image. Over time, things in the past get distorted and are quite different than they once were. The emotions that are associated with them weigh us down and get heavier as time goes on.

◆ If I spend too much time looking in the mirror, I lose my focus and run into the tree in front of me or off the road. So I have to remember to focus on the road ahead, no matter how tempting it is to look into the mirrors.

◆ The mirror serves a purpose, though, as it allows you to know what is behind you. The past is a training ground for the future, but only if you keep it in perspective. Learning from the past and not forgetting it is an important part of traveling light. If I forget my lessons of the past, they will hit me from behind when I'm not looking. If I forget to look into the mirror when I'm riding my bike, I may not move out of the way when I need to.

Lightening the load means putting those things from the past into their proper perspective. They are, after all, in the past and are useful as a frame of reference to help you create the better future. Your accomplishments and failures are a great springboard, so occasionally glance in the rear view mirror and the side mirrors, but keep most of your focus on the road ahead so you don't run into a tree.

Lightening the load means putting the future in perspective too. If your focus is too far ahead of you, you miss immediate opportunities and obstacles you need to notice along the way.

The Past ➜ Revisit It; Honor It; Let It Go
The Present ➜ Reconnect With It; Focus On It
The Future ➜ Keep It In Your Mind; Strive For It

The Light Pack

When preparing for a backpacking experience, you lay out everything you want to take with you...then you get rid of half of it...and then you get rid of everything else you don't need. It's tempting to take just one little thing that would be fun to have, such as the leather-bound journal, the extra underwear, or the large hairbrush, but you don't really need those things. Imagine how stupid I felt when I struggled to get to the Mt. Everest Base Camp, only to find in the bottom of my pack a lipstick weighing 14 ounces. Imagine how those 14 ounces would have impacted me when added to other needless things, like the leather-bound journal and the extra underwear.

After Tom passed away, I went kayaking in Alaska for a month. I slept on the beaches by night and kayaked in the beautiful Alaska wilderness by day. The weather was warm and rainy by day, then cold and rainy by night. Since I carried everything inside the hull of my kayak, I had to take as little as possible and still stay warm, dry, and well fed.

These are the clothes I took:

- 1 long underwear;
- 1 fleece layer;
- 1 wind layer;
- 1 outer fleece layer;
- 1 rain proof layer;
- 1 extra pair of underwear;
- 1 t-shirt (polypropylene).

I wore the same layers on the top and bottom, and was protected from the elements. The only extra clothing I had was the underwear and t-shirt, which I could wash every few days. I wore all these items all the time, even to bed. The first night I was cold and wet all the way through, despite the rain protection I was wearing. I crawled into my dry sleeping bag and nature took care of the rest. My body heat was trapped in the fleece layer and the rain layer, and within a half hour, I was totally dry, like a butterfly nestled snugly inside a cocoon.

I also took minimal food: simple dried vegetables, lots of light spices, pastas and rice, dried sauces, and tablets to treat the water. I had plenty to eat because I learned to cook creatively and simply. I ate only when I was hungry – eating only to live, not living to eat.

It was a simple life with few burdens. I focused on what was around me and lived in the present. It was a functional existence and left me open to see and experience everything I could. Unimportant burdens left me unencumbered and free to travel light… faster and easier.

During any transition, strip yourself of:

- Negative Relationships;
- Extra Stuff;
- Too Many Obligations;
- The Past.

And travel light. When you do:

- Your mind is free and open to all that is around you.
- You have more time to be connected to the positive people around you.
- You get the help and support you need.
- You lift your heart and free your spirit.
- You reflect and dig deep into your inner resolve and strength.
- You experience joyful moments.
- You follow your vision and passion.

Survival Tips

◈**Simplify.** Think of the things you carry with you. What can you unload? Make a list of all the things you don't need. At my workshops, I have people write these things on separate pieces of paper and then trash them. You'll be surprised how freeing it is to symbolically throw this stuff away once and for all.

◈**Stop worrying.** If you are a worrier and find it hard to get rid of burdens, ask for help from others. You can even ask for professional help. Sometimes a person with an objective point of view will help you to gain a healthy perspective.

◈**Set your sights forward, not backward.** Remember to look ahead, not behind you. Look at the road ahead and envision the top of your mountain. Then, set your small steps (goals) along the way to help you get there.

> THE PAST .. revisit it .. honor it .. learn from it .. **Let it go.**
> THE PRESENT .. concentrate on it .. focus on it .. and then **Live in the now.**
> THE FUTURE ... keep it in your mind .. strive for it .. and **Keep it in your heart.**

◈**Assess your relationships** and determine who your "yes" people are. If you feel comfortable, let the "no" people know you can't handle them right now. I never had the courage to do that, so I just let those relationships fade out. Funny how more "yes" people showed up during my grief process. Today I have a group of wonderful new friends.

◈**Make lists.** Writing lists of daily duties and obligations will help you keep on track and avoid cluttering your day with too much, which could cause you to lose focus.

◈**Rid your schedule of unnecessary obligations.** What have you said "yes" to that makes your life cluttered and unmanageable? Attend to the necessary responsibilities and delegate the rest to others.

◈**Clean your closets and your office.** Uncluttering your physical surroundings will unclutter your head and leave you open to possibilities.

Chapter Six

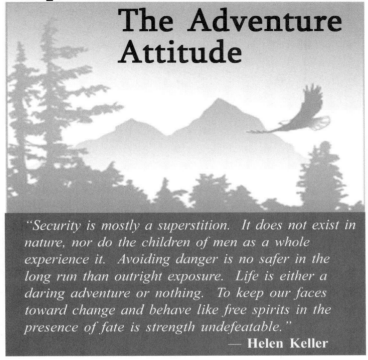

The Adventure Attitude

"Security is mostly a superstition. It does not exist in nature, nor do the children of men as a whole experience it. Avoiding danger is no safer in the long run than outright exposure. Life is either a daring adventure or nothing. To keep our faces toward change and behave like free spirits in the presence of fate is strength undefeatable."

— Helen Keller

We have talked about physical and intellectual preparedness. **The adventure attitude is about mental preparation.** It's about climbing with an optimistic, energetic, creative, and child-like attitude.

Attitude of Change

Everything in your life has changed, so it's not surprising that your attitude is different, too. You are not, and never will be, the same as you were before. The way you look at things is different now. During my grief process I became cynical for the first time in my life. The fact that I had a "reality check" made me take off the rose-colored glasses and put on the real ones – bifocals fitted for near- and far-sightedness. Those glasses had to be set for my new vision of the world.

Our individual views of the world and **how we react to the mountains are determined by all the things that make up who we are, including:**

◈ **Genetics** – the traits we were born with that determine our behavior and what we're like;

◈ **Family** – the initial environment we are born into that shapes our first view of the world;

◈ **Society and Culture** – the country and city we are a part of, or the extended environment that changes us as time goes on;

◈ **Events** – the things that affect our lives and slowly mold us;

◈ **Decisions We Make** – the right and wrong choices we make shape each day, as do how we deal with those decisions and how we learn from them (or not).

When major change occurs, and the "bomb goes off," your foundation is shaken. Your belief system is compromised. Everything you have learned has different meaning now. The way you react to things may be different, too. Certainly, losing a loved one or a job wipes out your belief in the natural order of things: people are not supposed to lose a loved one prematurely; people are not supposed to lose a job if they have done their best and worked hard; people are not supposed to lose their health if they have taken care of themselves.

The reality is that things do change, almost constantly. Usually we experience small changes that require a simple adjustment. Sometimes, however, the change is major, and your perception of the world determines how you react. That perception is determined by the attitude you were born with, which is altered by all the things that have happened, people you have been in contact with, and events that have shaped your life.

You can choose how you perceive things and how you react to them. It's your choice to take the things from the past, use them, and then surpass them by moving up the mountain.

Getting from the past to the future means seeing the mountain in your way—that obstacle you've been given—facing it, climbing it, learning from it, and using it to help you redefine yourself and open yourself up to new possibilities. **Recreation** is defined in the dictionary as "physical and mental refreshment." So **climbing the mountain is a way to re-create yourself actively.**

Your attitude determines where you go from here: Up, down, around, through, or nowhere but here. **The adventure attitude says you can climb the mountain if you look at it as an adventure. You do that by:**

◆ Facing the mountain and deciding to move on and climb it;

◆ Having a peak in your view and always looking up;

◆ Taking some risk, facing obstacles, and learning from them;

◆ Taking one step at a time … but still moving;

◆ Throwing the rope to others for help and emotional support;

◆ Using what you have used to benefit others.

The Adventure Attitude

The adventure attitude is not just a mountain climbing process; it is about a lifestyle choice. It's how you define yourself, your life, the world around you, and your circumstances.

As social creatures, we often let society define us. When I tell people I'm 60 years old, they say, "Ohhhhhh, you're 60!" as if to throw me prematurely into a wheelchair and send me down the ramp to the nursing home. Their reaction says, "You're reeeeelllly old; you're over the hill; the end is near; your life should be quiet and dull."

But the fact is, I define 60; they don't! Life for me is stress-free and I can have fun every day if I want to. I can choose what I do. My children are grown and out of the nest. I'm not financially responsible for them. My struggles are as hard as I want to make them. I have choices that others don't. I may not have much money, but I certainly can find a way to make it with what I have. I have learned many lessons, and I have paid my dues. Life is a wonderful adventure.

You have a choice about how you view your life. Change and climbing a mountain are hard if you think:

❖ I can't do it;

❖ I have too far to go;

❖ It will be too painful;

❖ It will be tedious;

❖ It's too much work;

❖ I'm happy here in bed;

❖ I love misery;

❖ I liked what I had before and
I won't change.

You will have a hard time climbing, because your heart won't be in it.

The adventure attitude is:

❖ Being positive in the face of the negative;

❖ Living in the moment with passion
and energy;

❖ Accepting the mountain and the challenge;

❖ Attempting to do something that may be
hard;

❖ Taking a little risk sometimes and opening
up personal boundaries;

❖ Seeing a world of possibilities;

❖ Living life to the fullest;

❖ Feeling your heart beat a little faster with
excitement and joy.

The result of living with the adventure attitude is personal balance, joy, and a life of possibility.

Think Like A Child

The adventure attitude is about looking at life much like a child looks at it. Imagine the toddler: Teetering on shaky legs and holding onto the couch with one hand, he sees something across the room that he wants. He lets go with the steadying hand. With one shaky step after the other, and eyes firmly glued onto prize, he goes for it. Suddenly, he plops down on his firmly padded butt. With what looks like a lot of effort, he gets up and starts again. If the prize becomes way too challenging, he refocuses on another object and tries for that, changing direction and focus.

The whole time the child is excited and positive, rarely discouraged by defeat. He is flexible enough to change focus and sees possibilities in every direction. His options are open. He doesn't think about defeat or pleasing someone else. The fire in his eyes and energy in his step tell it all. Life is a fun game, and anything in his path can become part of the game.

When a young child colors in a coloring book, she colors outside the lines, paying little attention to where the crayon goes. She uses her own choice of colors and knows she is creating a masterpiece. It's only when we adults tell her the real color of grass and show her how to color between the lines that her work of art changes. When we set the boundaries for the child, her creativity is stifled and she stops thinking like a child.

This thinking is reinforced in our schools when we teach the children that there is a right or wrong answer to most questions. When we slap our criteria of judgment on them with a grading system that compares them to other students in the class, we teach them to judge themselves and others. When they judge others, they become competitive. So much for innocence of unbridled creativity!

The Difference Between a Child and Me

I look at a field of dandelions and see a potential weed invasion. I see the yellow heads turning into the puffballs that will send seeds all over my yard. I see hours of work, killing them, digging them up, and moving them away.

My child sees them as beautiful flowers. He sees them as puffballs ready to blow and watch as they parachute up and then down. He hopes the yard will be full of them so he can have more fun.

I sing a song and am afraid of singing off tune or not singing the right notes. I don't want to look stupid so I sing only in the shower when no one else is home.

My child sings loud and strong, with reckless abandon. She could care less if someone is listening and judging.

I see a mud puddle in the driveway and walk around it. I want to get rid of it so no one will step in it. I don't want people to stomp mud into the house or get mud on their clothes.

My child stomps in the mud puddle and plays in it. He builds a lake resort by putting sticks together and building houses around it or reroutes it into a beautiful river. He sees endless possibilities of what that puddle can become.

The adventure attitude is all about thinking like a child and living with reckless abandon. It's about:

◈ Not being afraid of making mistakes;

◈ Appreciating life moment by moment;

◈ Seeing possibilities everywhere;

◈ Putting energy into every endeavor;

◈ Focusing on what you want;

◈ Having confidence;

◈ Having fun.

The Climbing Frame of Mind

When you have a mountain in your path, you have three choices:

1) Climb it,

2) Stand there and look at it, or

3) Retreat.

We all desire to ascend the mountain—to improve ourselves and to get out of bad situations. But most of us know it will be frightening and hard work. We could fail and we may get hurt. Something inside of each of us tells us to proceed with caution, or not to proceed at all.

"One can never consent to creep when one feels an impulse to soar." — **Helen Keller**

Look at the business world. All businesses want to evolve, compete, and increase the bottom line. Look at people, too. We all want to get through the transitions of our lives and find stability again. It's during these times of change and transition when we have the choice: climb the mountain, stay where we are, or quit and give up on life. You can either be an ascender, a camper, or descender.

Ascenders will go for the peak. These are the people with the adventure attitude.

◈They see the mountain in their path and want to climb it.

◈They live life fully, experience a major change and see it as an opportunity for adventure.

◈They actually seek challenge, see an obstacle in their path and take responsibility for it, by confronting it head on.

◈If they aren't successful, they learn from their mistakes and move on ... only to climb again.

◈They don't blame others for their situations or criticize, because they are too busy moving up and out, putting the past in proper perspective.

◈After time, they develop resiliency and strength.

◈They believe that anything is possible, and that in the end they *will* succeed.

In a business situation, these are the leaders who pull the company out of a bad situation, or the workers who do what they can to help and jump on board when changes are introduced.

In grief and transition, these are the people who take care of themselves and then work feverishly to make a new life.

Campers will not climb. They play it safe and stay where they are.

◈These are the people who set up camp and learn to be comfortable where they are, even if they are really miserable.

◈They often fear failure.

◈They remember how hard it was to get to the camp, so they become satisfied being there.

◈They often sit and wait for things to happen and are reluctant to make an effort.

◈These are the procrastinators who want to climb, but put it off as long as possible, so they become comfortable just sitting in the camp talking to everyone else.

◆ They make up a majority of the population.

In business situations, these are the people who take a "wait and see" attitude when the company is going through change. They love things the way they are and are happy with the status quo.

In grief and transition, these people become resigned to the situation and have trouble moving on. Sometimes, they need to wait and ascend later.

Descenders do not climb; they retreat.

◆ They flee from the situation.

◆ They go into denial and stay there.

◆ When life throws them challenges, and it's either fight or flight, they choose flight.

◆ They believe life is "closed" for them and there is no way out.

In business situations, these people resist and reject change, no matter what it is. Instead of working with the situation, or waiting to see what the future brings, they immediately reject it all.

In grief and transition their reaction is the same. They run away from it all.

No matter what your climbing frame of mind is, grief and change give you the opportunity to make the choice. Will you ascend, camp, or descend? It is your chance to redefine how you react to mountains in your path.

Glass Half Full or Glass Half Empty

Is the glass half full or half empty for you? It's actually both! The difference is how we choose to perceive the water in the glass. Some of us look at life for the content that is there, and some of us look at what isn't there.

Glass Half Full

The "half full" perception belongs to the optimists among us. They feel that bad things are isolated events and will pass. They feel that *what is* is not their fault, and they can learn from them and move on.

The dictionary definition of optimism is: "A doctrine that this world is the best possible world," and "An inclination to anticipate the best possible outcome of actions or events." In other words, the optimists really believe they are in control ... no matter what happens, they have a positive spin to it. Optimists tend to cope with stress and have a strong social network.

The Healthy Optimist ...	The Unhealthy Optimist ...
Sees possibilities where there are challenges.	Sees things unrealistically.
Sees positive where there is negative.	Sees through a rose-colored cloud.
Has a positive spin on life.	May be a Pollyanna and in denial.

Glass Half Empty

The pessimist sees the same situation as the optimist, yet he or she will see the negative in it. The dictionary definition of pessimism is: "An inclination to take the worst possible view of events or to expect the worst possible outcome." The pessimist complains and blames others or themselves for what's wrong. If something bad happens to pessimists, they assume it will take over their whole life and that they are helpless to do anything about it. They actually search out the negative spin on situations.

The Healthy Pessimist ...	The Unhealthy Pessimist ...
Sees the negative in situations and that changes can be made to improve them. Keeps the negative in perspective.	Sees hopelessness and the negative in everything in the present and in the future. Has a "gloom and doom" outlook and sees no way out of the negative situation.

The world is made up of both optimists and pessimists. **A balance of the healthy aspects of both shows us an authentic, real environment where positive change is able to take place.** During the stressful times of transition, however, whatever positive or negative traits an individual possesses intensify and may become destructive: the optimist may put on "the rose-colored glasses" of unreality, and the pessimist may be paralyzed in severe negativity.

Your attitude in transition, however, affects your reality. **If you are an optimist, you are more likely to be happy, have a social support group, and be in control of your life.** At the beginning of my own transition process, I was in "la la land," acting as if life was going on as usual and that I was "just fine." But as time passed, reality crept in little by little, and with it, my healthy optimism returned. I was able to see hope where there was none before. Eventually I was able to be happy and allow positive change to take place. Life actually became enjoyable. A positive, hopeful attitude leads to positive hopeful change.

Once You Think You Can Climb the Mountain, You Can!

Your attitude is your choice. Even if you consider yourself a negative person, you can learn to be more optimistic and less pessimistic. Just as you can learn to be helpless, you can learn to be in control of your life. No, you won't change your attitude overnight. But if you're aware of how you view your life, you can replace negative thoughts with positive ones. It's a necessary part of preparing to climb the mountain.

Doctors Avi Karni and Leslie Underleiden at the National Institutes of Mental Health found that regular repetition and practice of a task actually changes the physical-neural connections involved. So **if you are a pessimist, practicing a positive attitude may actually change the way you think.**

> *"... I think that as time goes on, you can make positive changes. Every day as soon as you get up, you can develop a sincere positive motivation, thinking, 'I will utilize this day in a more positive way.'"*
> — **The Dalai Lama**

The Dalai Lama suggests you can develop a positive attitude by keeping the intention close to mind and checking in the evening to see how you've done. With regular practice, you can strengthen the positive aspects of your mind and thus control your habits of thinking negatively.

In *Man's Search for Meaning* by Victor Frankl, we see vividly how some of the prisoners in the German concentration camps survived. He said it was all about their attitude:

"We who lived in concentration camps can remember the men who walked through the huts comforting others, giving away their last piece of bread. They may have been few in number, but they offer sufficient proof that everything can be taken from a man but one thing: the last of human freedoms ... the freedom to choose your attitude in any given set of circumstances, to choose your own way.

"And there are always choices to make. Every day, every hour, offered the opportunity to make a decision, a decision which determined whether you would or would not submit to those powers which threatened to rob you of your very self, your inner freedom: which determined whether or not you would become a plaything of circumstance, renouncing freedom and dignity to become molded into the form of the typical inmate. ... any man, therefore, can under any circumstances decide what shall become of him mentally and spiritually."

Attitude and Stress

Attitude is directly related to stress, especially during grief and change. Pessimism is more stressful than optimism. Studies show that a negative attitude results in stress and poor mental and physical health, while a positive, optimistic attitude can improve your immune system and actually extend your life.

Clinical tests prove that physically, stress fills the body with stress toxins and free radicals. Your brain, in turn, accelerates your heart rate and tenses your sphincter muscles to prepare you for fight or flight. Your blood speeds towards your muscles and away from your brain and digestive tract. You may have trouble thinking clearly, become mentally "stuck," and have digestive problems. Your nutrition is compromised, as is your energy and ability to cope with daily pressures.

A 20-year Mayo Clinic study (1962 – 1982) concluded that those who rate high in pessimism are much more likely to die prematurely than those who rate high in optimism. The way people describe stressful events in their lives affects their physical and mental health, and an optimistic approach to life can improve the course of an illness.

In a report, Dr. Andrew Weil described the physical effects of stress as:

◈Digestive symptoms;
◈Headaches;
◈Chronic pain;
◈Muscular pain;
◈Skin problems;
◈Insomnia;
◈Anxiety;
◈Depression;
◈Frequent infection.

Clearly, grief and transition are critical times of stress. Approaching it with a positive attitude may help you weather the storm ... and choose to climb the mountain.

Survival Tips

❖ **Reduce stress.** Do whatever you need to in order to reduce stress. Stay away from negative things and people; seek positive friends, keep busy, exercise, and do fun recreational activities.

❖ **Try new things.** Think of some fun, low-cost things you can do that you enjoy. Honor yourself by making time to do something just for you ... alone. Try to think like a child with a full world of possibility from which to choose.

❖ **Be fully present** and notice how you approach life – positively or negatively. Once you notice when you are negative, change that mindset once a day. Increase the frequency of that change little by little, day-by-day. You will be amazed at how much better you feel, and how people react to you.

❖ **Create a gratitude journal.** Positive thinking becomes natural for you when you think about what you are grateful for. Every evening, make a list of all the things you are grateful for. You will find that the more you write, the more you will think in the positive. Example: "I am grateful for a beautiful cool morning, the flowers in my garden, the promise of rain, the smile on the face of the little boy I saw this morning, and the nice man I talked to in the coffee shop." Keep it simple. It will change your thinking.

❖ **Affirmations.** I've mentioned this technique before, but it's critical that you say positive, uplifting, present tense statements frequently. Write a note to yourself with your affirmations on it and tape it on your mirror. When you look ridiculous, smiling at yourself in the mirror, you can remind yourself how awesome you are.

❖ **Try an attitude readjustment.** Notice the good in things and ask yourself, "What am I supposed to learn from this?" Make a list of some of the bad things that have happened to you. Then, write how that changed your life for the good and what you learned from it. This will help you change your mindset.

❖**Fake it till you make it.** This may sound odd, but when you get up in the morning, look in the mirror. Put the biggest smile on your face, and hold it for at least ten seconds. Do it again several times during the day, especially when you find a negative thought creeping in. Surprisingly, you will find that happiness follows you when you start with a smile and positive thoughts.

❖**Do the Dalai Lama Attitude check.** In the morning, think of positive attitude intentions for the whole day. Check in the evening to see how you did. Did you approach your moments of the day with a positive frame of mind? Keeping your intentions close to mind peaks your awareness of how you approach life.

❖**Reframe your attitude.** Think of how you can reframe your challenges into something positive:

FROM:	I lost my job	I hate the company. I hate my boss. I got jipped. Life always does this to me. I'm lousy, but they're all worse.
TO:	I lost my job	There's nothing I can do about it; what's done is done. This is my chance to find something I LOVE to do. I don't have to put up with my boss anymore. I'm lucky to be free.
FROM: I lost my spouse		I can't live without him/her. I won't make it through the day. I'm miserable.
TO: I lost my spouse		He/She is with me in spirit. I can make it through the day if I take it moment by moment. I'm miserable, but I will be stronger as time goes on. I have nowhere to go but up.

Chapter Seven

Climbing out of the Comfort Zone

"Why not go out on the limb? That's where the fruit is!" — **Will Rogers**

Climbing the mountain is scary for most. We know it will be hard and that we may fail. That's why **climbing is about stretching out of the familiar and taking some risks.** As a family, we learned about risk from a nature experience we had while on a family vacation.

Lessons From the Eagle

One year our family planned a canoe trip in the Quetico Wilderness of Canada, just north of Ely, Minnesota. Tom was the trip organizer and, being the paramount adventurer, decided that 31 portages were the perfect number for our young family of three boys, aged 8, 11, and 13.

(Portaging involves carrying the canoes, food, tents, and all clothes and equipment from one body of water to another. Sometimes it's a short distance and you can see your destination. Other times, it might require a two-mile trek through mud or trees, or scrambling over logs. Two miles becomes six if you have to return for a second load.)

In the beginning, things went smoothly. The paddling was easy, and we quickly devised a successful portage strategy and system. Tom, being the macho guy, would take a canoe on his head all by himself. The two oldest boys, in an effort to also appear tough and manly, would take the other canoe. I would take a heavy pack, and Chris, my youngest, would carry another.

The trail was often mosquito-ridden and swampy, and the two boys, with their heads in the canoe, would be slapping their legs, losing their balance and stumbling over logs, and often landing in a muddy puddle. I was shocked to hear the expletives coming out of the mouths of my "innocent babies." Meanwhile, Chris and I followed, struggling under the weight of our heavy backpacks. Then, we had to repeat the entire exercise to pick up the remaining load. The older boys and Dad would reluctantly shoulder the tent and food packs, and I would masterfully beat out Chris for the prize load—the paddles.

On one very tough day, we'd had several long portages prior to landing at our campsite. By the time we arrived, we were all exhausted and upset with each other. The boys were mad at Tom for arranging such a hard trip and mad at me for going along with it. The boys were mad at each other for just being alive. No one talked. And nobody would budge … except Tom, who quickly made a fire and started dinner.

In the absolute silence, we heard the sound of sticks falling onto the rocks around us. Then we noticed small, white feathers floating through the air. We looked up and saw a huge mother eagle, way up in her nest, throwing debris out to the ground below. Also in the nest were two eaglets. The adult male eagle paced back and forth on the beach below and kept looking up as if waiting for something to happen.

We found out later what the female was doing to the nest. She was picking out all the cushy, comfy parts of the nest and throwing them to the ground below. Occasionally, she would grasp the nest with her talons and shake it furiously. Eventually, all that was left of the nest were the intertwined, pointy sticks.

Soon, the eaglets, who found the sticks just too painful to sit on, moved to the edge of the nest. Then, the mother picked up the eaglet closest to her and in a flurry of wing-thrashing, threw it out of the nest. The terrified eaglet flapped its wings furiously … with absolutely no effect.

Suddenly, the male took flight to directly beneath the eaglet and supported it as it crash-landed into a tree, landing on a branch. Father and son stood together, while junior plucked up the courage to try again. With another great flurry of wings, it was off again, accompanied by the father until it landed ungracefully on a branch. Over the next few tries, the eaglet flew progressively better. Then, quite by accident, it faced into the wind. Miraculously, it opened its wings and effortlessly glided off the branch. It had graduated from flight school!

The eaglet discovered that if he took the leap and relaxed, what he needed to survive would be given to him.

◈ He had the instincts he needed all along; instincts that told him the thermal wind currents would surely hold him up.

◈ He didn't fear failure, or under estimate himself.

◈ He focused on what he knew he had to do, and didn't depend on others to do it for him.

◈ He relied on his own strength because he was prepared and knew his muscles were strong enough to carry him where he was supposed to go.

◈ He had to take the risk, give up control, listen to his encouragers, and follow the beating of his own heart.

I'm not sure whether the eagles touched the boys like they touched me, but I'm sure nature will teach them what they are supposed to learn if they just look up, watch, and listen. Isn't that true for all of us?

When Tom died a few years after that vacation, I found out what it was like to be that eaglet sitting on the prickly sticks. I was pushed off the nest, not by a mother eagle, but by the hand fate had dealt me. I had no choice but to jump off the edge into a brand new life. At first I flapped my wings and got nowhere. I was terrified that I would fail and felt lost and alone. But like the eaglet, taking the risk and facing the challenge taught me a lot.

And this is what I learned….

◈ **You must have courage.** It's tough to stand on the edge and take the leap into the unknown, but sometimes you have to do it. And you need to expand and grow when things get a little too comfortable.

◆**You must have love, for yourself and others.** You may not fly with your wings touching, but you need to have your hearts touching so you fly the same direction. You need to stay together and help each other, especially during those times when you step out into the unknown.

◆**You must have faith,** so that you can trust enough to open your wings and ride the thermal currents. You also must realize that you are part of something larger than yourself. Call it God, the spiritual world, or the universe. We all are part of it, and it will help us up when we start to fall.

Taking risks is a part of every big change. Whether you've experienced the loss of a loved one, a job loss, or disappointment or change of any kind, that fear of failing, feeling pain, getting hurt, and jumping into the unknown is always present. Your security has been compromised and you are out of your comfort zone. Eventually you must follow your instincts that tell you nothing stays the same, and you must take the risk and change as your situation has changed. You must face the fear of the unknown and step out of the comfort zone.

Jumping out of the comfort zone and taking risk does amazing things. It:

◆ Shows you a world of possibilities;

◆ Gives you confidence to try new things all the time;

◆ Opens up your creativity;

◆ Helps you see things differently;

◆ Gives you energy;

◆ Replaces pain with new learning;

◆ Expands who you are.

I found a poem that now has a permanent home on my refrigerator. I look at it frequently to remind myself what a gift it is to learn to take risks.

RISKS

When you get hooked on risk, your whole life changes ...
To laugh is to risk appearing the fool
To weep is to risk appearing sentimental
To reach out for another is to risk involvement
To place your ideas, your dreams before a crowd is to
risk being called naïve
To love is to risk not being loved in return
To live is to risk dying
To hope is to risk despair
To try is to risk failure
But risks must be taken, because the greatest risk in life
is to risk nothing!
The person who risks nothing, does nothing, has
nothing, is nothing and becomes nothing
He may avoid suffering and sorrow, but he cannot learn,
and feel, and change, and grow, and love and live.
Chained by his servitudes, he is a slave. He has forfeited
his freedom.
ONLY THE PERSON WHO RISKS IS FREE!
— **Author Unknown**

Facing Fear

The wilderness taught me much about fear. The challenge of
overcoming the mountain, physically and mentally, making it
day-to-day, and overcoming obstacles along the way are much
like normal life.

Standing on the ledge, gripped with fear, and trying to move
on is like those times when we must do something difficult. We
are afraid to try for fear we will fail ... or are afraid of being
stuck right where we are.

Struggling up the trail step by painful step, fearing that if
we don't take the next step, we won't make it, is like those
times when we are stuck in the daily drudgery of life. We don't
like it, but we fear that if we skip a step, we will fail.

Fear wears two faces. It can lock us in an invisible prison
or it can be a motivator that alerts us to possible danger. Fear
can stop us from moving ahead, leaving us where we are, afraid

to move either direction. Or fear can help us to mobilize the resources we need to protect ourselves and push us out of the comfort zone. It alerts us into "fight or flight" or to do something we never thought we could do just to survive. Fear can motivate us to discover things about ourselves that we wouldn't have discovered had we not been forced to. Fear can teach us how to manage ourselves by showing us what our personal boundaries are.

The fear of not being able to provide for your family in a financial crisis can motivate you to find a new direction for your career. The fear of not making it alone can be the resulting pain of being stuck and lost ... and can motivate you to love being alone.

Life in the Comfort Zone

All our lives, we search for two things: love and security. **We like our comfort zones because we feel safe there, and we know that life is predictable.** Going through change challenges that security. That's why people often stay in jobs they hate or marriages that are harmful. That's why people have trouble quitting smoking or become alcoholics. Even if the situation is negative, at least it's something familiar.

The unknown is fraught with fear. It brings with it a sense of being out of control. We feel powerless. That's when we need courage. **Courage means facing the challenge and the fear connected with it, putting the fear aside, and replacing it with hope.** With faith in God (or a Higher Power) and friends who support us, we are able to jump, knowing that if things don't get better, they will at least be different.

What stops us from taking risks?

◈**We fight ourselves,** saying that we won't be able to adjust and will surely fail. We are afraid that if we succeed, we have to think differently and put the past behind us. We stop ourselves from taking risk.

◈**We listen to others who put limits on us and tell us not to try.** We give power to others to decide what is best for us. Their decisions are based on their criteria of judgment, not ours.

Where does the fear come from?

◈**Who we are.** The traits we were born with, and the family environment that shaped us, have created a deeply ingrained set of behaviors and boundaries. Going against the grain ... pushing those comfort levels beyond what we are used to ... is hard and painful. If we are used to the status quo and are happy that way, it's tough to take chances that may shake that foundation. If we are risktakers by nature and grew up looking at life from *outside* the comfort zone, it's easier for us.

◈**Our past experiences teach us lessons by which we live.** Over time, we find out what works and what doesn't work. We learn to adjust, slowly but surely. We adjust to what we have, where we are, and who we are with. Going outside the comfort zone and trying new things is like charting new territory. We have lessons to learn from each success and failure. Taking risks means being willing to be on shaky ground until we find our way again.

◈**Society conditions us** by telling us what we should and shouldn't do. Our cultural environment dictates our behavior. Deviation from these unwritten values and expected conduct result in disdain and ridicule. For example, standards say how fast we should make major decisions during the grief process. While we should consider those standards, we should not live by them.

We are all different and, like the eagle, we must **rely on our own instincts.** By following the inner voice that tells you "try this" or "go this way," you find a path. Other cues along the way tell us when to change the path and go another way.

While I was in transition, people criticized me for selling my house in four months. The truth is, I had to move on. My financial survival depended on it. I gained nothing by stalling the move. My survival instincts told me to move ahead. For some people, this would not have been the best thing to do, but I followed my *own* instincts and did what I had to. My life became simpler and more efficient as a result of that move. I made room for new things to come in.

"There is a vitality, a life force, an energy, a quickening, that is translated through you into action, and because there is only one of you in all time, this expression is unique. If you block it, it will never exist through any other medium..." — **Martha Graham Dancer**

Weighing the Options
During transition, we are especially vulnerable. We are on shaky ground, unsure of who we are, where we're going, and what to do next. We have two ways to look at our situation:

◈ **What happens if I don't take the risk?** Will I be even *more* unstable, stuck where I am, and feel more pain? Will I regret it?

◈ **If I take the risk, what will happen if I fail?** Will I inflict more pain on myself? Will I regret it?

Going out of the comfort zone can change our view of life. Just like the eaglet, the safety and comfort of the nest give way to new life. We learn:

- That things will always be different;
- That a world of possibilities we haven't even tried awaits us;
- That our lives are forever enriched;
- That there are different ways to define success;
- That some things work and other don't for us;
- That risk gets easier and easier to take;
- That the comfort zone expands in size.

"I choose to inhabit my days, to allow my living to open me, to make me less afraid, more accessible, to loosen my heart until it becomes a wing, a torch, a promise ..."
— **Dawna Markova**

Risk = Reward

My friend Keith was a successful engineer and vice president of his company. His definition of success was "boosting the bottom line" for his company by increasing productivity, and thus making more money for his family. When he lost his job and the company went bankrupt, he lost his income, savings, pension, and retirement plan. In transition, Keith struggled to find a new life for himself and his family. Eventually he took a risk, jumped into something new and found a new way of looking at success. He got a job using his skills to help victims of natural disasters. Now he finds profound satisfaction in making a meaningful contribution to the lives of others. His definition of success has changed, and he is extremely happy and fulfilled. So is his family.

The Mind/Body Connection

The body and mind work together to help you take necessary risks. When fear takes over, your body releases endorphins, which dull physical and emotional pain while they shoot to your brain and make your blood pump a little faster. They drive you to feats of athleticism you have never known before, push you to make the next step, and move you out of the comfort zone. They cause you to become intensely focused and clear-headed when you need it most.

Stuck on the Rock Face

Several years ago I climbed a 14,500-foot peak in Colorado called Uncompadre Peak. I was climbing with ten young people. We started our ascent at about 3 am so we would be at the peak for sunrise. Most of the climb was on narrow paths. It was a hard hike but didn't require any technical skill.

About 6:30 am, just as the sun was about to rise, I came to a sheer face of rock … and I mean *sheer … straight up*. I had no technical equipment and it looked like something I wasn't mentally or physically qualified to do. My intuition told me, "Stop and wait here for the rest to come back down … you don't have to prove anything to anyone."

Just as I was settling in on a small ledge, looking down into the rest of the world, a young man came up from the rear … the last one in the group. He told me, "After you get past that

75-foot rock face, it's only 100 yards to the peak." So instead of listening to myself, I listened to him ... and started to climb up the face.

Suddenly fear gripped me and I did the worst possible thing a climber can do – I looked down. I lost my footing and ended up hanging onto a rock with one arm. My other hand gripped onto a crevice in the rock. I started to whimper. The guy behind me had to calm me down.

He said, "Don't worry ... you'll be fine ... if you fall, I can catch you." I knew in my heart that if I fell, we would both die, but I wanted to believe him. He continued, "Don't look down. Just raise your right foot up about six inches and four inches to the right and you'll find a place for your foot. Then, right above that, to the left, is a place for your other foot. Then you're on your way."

I panicked. Why hadn't I listened to myself in the first place? At least, I was awake now and I listened carefully, not only to him, but also to myself. I got outside my body, breathed deeply, assessed the situation, and dug deep inside to find the courage to push up. Without thinking, I was suddenly at the top and got to see the sunrise.

I learned a big lesson that day: When we run into obstacles, we need each other. But more than anything, we need to breathe, step back, assess, dig deep within ... and go for it. We can't change the fact that the rock is there. We can only take these times to find our own resources. Facing the obstacles, breathing, stepping back, looking for the familiar, listening to our intuition, and proceeding slowly and deliberately is the only way to overcome our fear.

Courage

"Courage is resistance to fear ... mastery of fear ... not absence of fear." — **Mark Twain**

We often think of superheroes as the fictional embodiment of courage, as they face challenges without fear and forge ahead into dangerous situations without concern for life and limb. I think of my friend Jack who, at age 70, bungee jumps off bridges and ledges and hang-glides from cliffs. He looks like a super hero to me.

In reality, in daily life, the person with courage is much more than that. He faces challenges by resisting outside pressure and doing what he thinks is right. She supports the unpopular position if it's morally right and resists pressure to take the easy way out. He follows a strong value system, supporting others when it's hard, and taking care of his family above all else.

This does not mean she lives without fear. It doesn't mean that she goes through tough times and isn't afraid of the consequences of taking risks. Instead, she has the fortitude, or strength of mind, that allows her to endure the pain and go on anyway, taking the risks necessary to travel outside the comfort zone.

So where do you get the courage to get through these challenging times? Courage is hidden deep inside each of us, just as the seed is hidden in the cone. **Going through transition is not for sissies,** for at every turn of the road, it seems the comfort zone doesn't even exist. Stability and comfort come in time. Like the eaglet that flaps courageously trying to find its soaring altitude, you will find the courage to stick it out and find your zone.

It takes courage...

To Live Fully ... enjoying the moments along the way;

To Be a Friend ... and stand by someone no matter what;

To Trust Someone ... even if he may be untrustworthy;

To Get Older ... and use your lessons to teach others;

To Retire ... and say goodbye to the life you knew;

To Face Death ... and yet affirm beauty and find joy in life;

To Do the Right Thing ... no matter what the consequences are;

To Support the Downtrodden ... even if there's nothing in it for you;

To Find a New Life ... even it will be painful;

To Love Fully ... even if you may get hurt.

Measured Risk

Imagine climbing a mountain without a map, or without your hiking boots. Taking risks for risks' sake is dangerous. Sometimes we try something risky before we are ready, and it can lead to disaster. **Remembering to "look before you leap" will stop you from crashing into a concrete wall.**

We've all taken foolish risks at one time. Once I climbed a mountain in Colorado without thinking it through, without the right equipment, without physical preparation, and even without a map. During transitions, I did a lot of running around, trying one adventure after another without really being fully prepared for any of them. Miraculously, I did them all without really getting hurt.

It was only when my psychologist friend asked me, "So, Cheryl, when do you think you will stop running away?" that I realized what I was actually doing. I wasn't filling myself with adventures for any reason but to get away from feeling the pain of grief. I took chances and made drastic changes so I wouldn't have to stand still and feel anything. **I was not moving towards a new life but away from reality.**

Fear diminishes as competence improves. The more confidence we gain, the more we venture out. As we prepare and practice, the risk becomes less and less. Measured risk is risk taken with careful forethought and preparation. After thinking it through, you may learn that you must wait before you take the leap. You may learn the risk is too great. You may learn what it takes to move out of the comfort zone.

Sometimes it takes more courage **not** to take risk. This is when you must:

◈ Work through what you have;

◈ Do what is right for yourself and your family;

◈ Be true to your value system;

◈ Follow through with your responsibilities;

◈ Do what you are physically and mentally qualified to do;

◈ Take the time to be totally prepared;

◈ Be patient.

The Back-Up Plan

The back-up plan is a soft pillow to fall into if things don't go the way you planned. When we are climbing a mountain, ropes connect each person for safety. If someone falls, the rope supports the weight and stops the fall. The climber is the risk-taker; the rope support system is the back-up plan.

Lessons from Prince Charming

Two-and-a-half years after I was widowed I had my first date. Since I hadn't dated in 32 years, it was a frightening experience. I'd heard many stories about sexual encounters on the first date, to say nothing of the innocent victims lying armless and legless in the streets of Chicago ... no doubt abandoned by a "first date."

With much fear and trepidation I agreed to meet the stranger I met in the Frankfurt airport for dinner. I don't know what I was thinking when I gave him my address and phone number. I certainly didn't have enough confidence to think he would ever call me when he passed through Chicago on business. But he did. So, I was stuck in a potentially dangerous situation, meeting with a man who could be a serial rapist or killer. And I didn't even remember what he looked like.

I immediately called a friend who had the means to do a little checking on who he really was, to find out whether he was who his business card said he was. Then I worked on making the perfect plans: park the car away from his hotel so I wouldn't have to walk *too* close to it en route to the parking garage; get the key to a friend's apartment so I could make a quick escape if need be; wear a conservative skirt with blazer; tell two people where I'm going and who with *just in case* they have to find me. It sure sounded like I covered my bases just fine.

I self-talked my way to the hotel, where I was to meet him, giving myself the caution and self-confidence lecture. I walked into the hotel, and there he was, looking just as if he'd stepped off his white horse ... handsome and confident. We went out for a fantastic dinner. I looked him right in the eyes and asked him about family – children and marital status – watching and searching for evidence of deception. I ended my first date with Prince Charming, making plans for date number two the next night.

The next night I let my guard down just a little bit, but told myself to be alert and careful not to drink too much wine. He pulled out all the stops that night, pouring out the charm and slowly, carefully, and masterfully guiding me into his web. And

I saw it coming. Such charm is a skill only the deceitful know. I laughed to myself as I pondered just how this suave mover-and-shaker would pop that question meant to get me into the hotel room.

Casually, he asked, "Say, would you like to come back to my room for a little drink?" A simple question ... but loaded with major content.

With my back-up plan securely nestled in my back pocket, I replied, "Sure, but only for a few minutes. And there will be some boundaries."

"Like what?" he asked.

"No sex," was my response.

"Okay."

Yeah, right, I thought. So off we went to his hotel room. All the way up the elevator, I laughed to myself and reminded myself that if I should end up legless and armless, or at the very least, raped, it would be my own fault.

On the table by the window was a bucket of ice, two glasses and a bottle of wine. He put his arms around me and prepared to capture me. I turned into him and out of the corner of my eye caught a glimpse of a photograph ... of a woman. His wife? "Oh, that must be your wife," I said.

He said no in a way I knew was a lie, so my turn became a 360, and without a word, I grabbed my purse and was out the door. I rushed to the car parked two blocks away, picked up my cell phone, and laughed as I told my friends about my first date in my new world.

My Backup Plan

When I went kayaking in Alaska on a solo adventure, I made sure someone knew my route, and checkpoints helped people keep track of where I was. When I took a job that I knew was pushing my boundaries beyond my ability level, I was sure to have experienced people to ask questions of. When I went to dinner alone, I was sure to have my cell phone with me so I could call someone if I got too lonely. Having someone or something to fall back on gives you that soft pillow. Just like the eagle, when you're standing on the ledge and you take the risk and jump, you know you will be okay if you are supported.

A back-up plan protects you and gives you the courage to try new things.

Failure

"Failure is the foundation of success, and the means by which it is achieved." — **Lao-Tzu**

Failure does not exist. Yet, failing is the one thing we fear the most. It is a concept forced on us by our culture and internalized by ourselves. The word "failure" implies judgment and suggests we are living our lives based on "shoulds" – we *should* behave in a certain way, we *should* get something done properly. And if we don't behave as we *should* and do things as we *should*, we have somehow failed.

Ideally, defining failure for ourselves opens up a world of possibilities. If we take a risk and the result is not what we think it *should* be, it is *not* failure as long as we learn from it. It is not failure if we learn what *doesn't* work and then do it again a different way the next time. It is not failure if we do the best we can, and fall short, because we have some great experiences to appreciate along the way. Setbacks lead to corrections, insights, and knowledge of our own strengths and weaknesses. Valuable delays lead to study, revised plans, and ultimately more chance of success.

I like to think of life as one great experiment. There are no failures, only results. Scientists *live* that way, every day. Experiments, failures, and successes along the way are how we have cured diseases and solved world problems. Failures lead to more chance of successes. For example, the Post-It Note resulted from a failed glue-making experiment, and penicillin was discovered when an experiment became contaminated.

Cheryl Lays an Egg

My new life led to a career as a speaker and writer. Clearly, speaking in front of an audience was one of those things I was once terrified of, but the grief process led me to use what I learned from nature and mountain climbing for the benefit of others. I was determined to get over that fear. Sure, I once laid an egg in public … in front of an audience. I was on the platform but *not* on the platform. I froze and stalled, and was in total agony and pain, but learned some amazing lessons. I was, at one moment, standing solidly on two feet, giving it my all and leading with my heart. Then, at the next moment, I lost my footing, my balance, and my touch with solid ground.

I was participating in a video showcase where I was giving a small speech that was being videotaped by a group of videographers. My intuition told me I was jamming too much into a busy week. I didn't listen. Instead, I forged ahead into the taping with the intention of telling snippets of personal mountain adventure stories I know well and tell often.

Lights, Camera, Action!

Before my turn, in a stall in the ladies room, I muttered lines under my breath. I did deep breathing exercises and all the visualizations in my personal arsenal, and then ended with a prayer. I prayed that whatever happened in front of the camera that day would teach me the lessons I needed to learn at this point in my fledgling speaking career and affirm that I am well on my way to a *great* speaking career ... *or* ...... (Oops, thinking the '*or*' inadvertently allowed the negative to creep in).

Before I knew it, it was my turn. I stood up on the stage, confident and comfortable with my script on the desk in front of me. Five sentences into my material, the videographer shouted. "Cut!" He needed to adjust the background. As he adjusted the background, I should have adjusted my foreground, but I didn't. Five sentences again, then, "Cut. Start again. The camera needs adjustment." He adjusted his camera, but I didn't make my mental adjustment. In mountain climbing I know there are sometimes unexpected distractions. Failure to adjust, readjust, and focus can cause loss of footing with serious consequences.

Encore

I started again and this time stumbled on my own words. That was the end, at least for me. I had allowed myself to lose my footing totally. Suddenly, I found myself robotically groping for the scripted material. My words lurched out of my mouth, and with every word, I fell further and further away from myself. My body got stiff and tense. I totally lost connection to my material and myself. I looked for help from the audience. Mercifully time finally ran out, and I was free.

Back to the bathroom! This time, however, I felt profound humiliation. I felt as if I'd totally lost myself. As a mountain climber, I know about balance: being centered with my feet solidly under me, focusing on short term goals, breathing to stay centered, and then traveling one careful step at a time. During the taping, I felt as if I were standing on one foot, on a narrow ledge, looking down, holding my breath, and waiting for the inevitable fall into the canyon. In my porcelain retreat, I felt injured and hurt, but grateful to be alive. Now, how could I pull myself back from the ledge and onto solid ground?

Empty Words

For a week I analyzed the experience and relived the humiliation of it. I had lost connection with the stories that were so much a part of my life. I spoke the words, but they had no meaning and became shallow and flat. Being out of balance was being out of relationship. It meant "playing a role" in a self-made plastic environment instead of speaking from my heart for the benefit of the audience.

However, before the event, I had prayed that whatever happened in front of the camera would teach me what I needed to learn at this point in my fledgling speaking career. I just didn't bargain for it being so painful.

I had laid an egg. Now I had a choice. I could throw it out of the nest and let it rot in a place where I would never see it again, or I could incubate it, fuss over it, and embrace it in hopes that it would hatch into new life and a new beginning. I chose the latter.

Back to Basics

Lessons from the mountain came back to me. "Failure" can be an opportunity to see things from a new perspective:

◈To regain balance means returning to basics, which starts within. Remember who you are, why you are doing what you are doing, what you value, and what your purpose is. Being authentic and real at all costs is the only way to connect with your material and believe in what you are doing so that you can stand on a solid base.

◈Remember to listen to your intuition. That inner voice is usually right. When you are true to that, you can embrace "pure commitment."

◈Prepare your material and prepare yourself. Know your own limits. Stretching is necessary to grow and improve. However, always sense how far you can stretch without breaking.

◈Stay awake and focused. Focusing forward and inside turns fear around and propels you ahead with greater force.

◈Remember the importance of relationships. The faces in the audience the day I laid my egg and the people I'm roped together with when I'm climbing up an ice field are there for mutual support. If I had taken the time to connect with them that day, I would have found my feet.

I really got what I prayed for in the bathroom before the video showcase. Just as the momentum of the roller coaster of my perceived failure pulled me crashing to the bottom of a steep hill, it sent me just as far up the other side. I learned that laying an egg can be painful but can also be a wonderful gift. I am a much better presenter and have much more to offer my clients because of it.

Survival Tips

❖ **List your successes.** Think of all the things you do right and what it was like to do them for the first time. Your comfort zone expands with the successes you have. Think of how big your comfort zone really is now. Define it and put your foot out of it, one toe at a time. It will get bigger and bigger.

❖ **Change some little things.** We certainly are creatures of habit. To change your mindset and see things creatively, change some of the small habits and routines. Sit in a different place at the table when you eat, drink coffee without reading the newspaper, take the dog for a walk around the block in the opposite direction, or go to a completely different place. It's amazing but you will find yourself opening yourself up to creative thinking. In my workshops on creative thinking, I find people come up with amazing creative solutions to problems if they just change some of these small habits.

❖ **Do something scary.** Think about what really frightens you, something that gives you a creepy feeling inside. Do that scary thing anyway. Take just the first small step. Have a back-up plan … tell people what you are doing, have them there for you … and then go for it.

❖ **Embark on a personal adventure.** Take yourself on adventures, big or small. Do it alone and regularly. Make sure it's something a little different from anything you have done before. Put it on the calendar so you don't find a way to get out of it. You'll likely think of every excuse in the book not to, but DO IT. Tell people you are doing it so you follow through. When you finish with one adventure, schedule the next one so you have something to look forward to. Take care of yourself now. It will make your heart beat a little faster and rejuvenate you.

❖**Have a back-up plan.** If you are afraid to make first step into new things, tell others, make sure you are prepared, and have a back-up plan so you feel safe. You'll find those attempts to move out of your comfort zone get easier and more successful every time.

❖**Honor who you are.** Make sure you listen to that inner voice that tells you how far you should go. It usually knows best.

❖**Analyze your fears.** Being in touch with what you are REALLY afraid of will help you put that fear into proper perspective

❖**Realize that failure does not exist.** We've all failed many times in our lives. Recheck those failures now. Were they lessons and gifts in disguise? What new beginnings came out of them? What lessons?

❖**Try to do things alone.** Try it little by little. There is no need to rush into it too quickly. Try something small at first, such as going to the movies. Once you get through the ticket line, you will be sitting in the dark, and are safe there. I found it to be a great way to get used to it.

❖**Have faith.** An unseen force always holds us up when we start to fall. Let go of control on things you can't control anyway, and have faith that you will be supported.

Chapter Eight

Climbing One Step at a Time

"Even a nine storied terrace began with a single basket of dirt. Even a 1000-mile journey began with a single step" — **Lao Tzu**

The helicopter left us at an airstrip in the town of Lukla, a small Sherpa village high in the Himalayas. It was nothing like the modern airports we are used to, but a small dirt runway surrounded by a few short dingy huts, with many Sherpas bustling around, smiling and chattering. It was a different world, so beautiful and yet primitive. This is where our adventure began.

The base camp of Mt. Everest was the destination we had imagined in our mind, but we had no idea what it would really be like. After several days of hiking on dirt trails that wound in and out of beautiful lush terraced valleys, we got our first glimpse of Mt. Everest way in the distance. Although the smaller peaks closer to us dwarfed it, we were awestruck by the vastness of it, given the distance from us. Then I was struck by the reality of the task before us.

Looking at the peak in the distance, I thought to myself: *There is no way I will be able to walk that far.* It looked totally unreachable.

I asked myself this question: If a helicopter were to pick me up and drop me off at the base camp, would I prefer that? Just think of all the things I would miss in between here and there – the beauty, the people I would meet along the way, the challenge, and the sense of accomplishment.

When my life changed and my readjustment process began, I faced another mountain far in the distance. I had to sell my house, sell my cars and my business, find a home for my dogs, find a place to live, and get a job. If I thought of all of these things together, in global terms, I was overwhelmed. It was like seeing Mt. Everest in the distance and knowing it was just too tough a challenge. I quickly learned to "chunk" or take each small challenge, one at a time. Then I was able to put them behind me one at a time and moved on to the next. Only then was the challenge do-able.

The grief process seems never-ending. I remember when I ran into a psychologist friend of mine in the second year. He told me that when you lose a loved one, the grief process takes five to seven years. "Five to seven years!" I exclaimed. "Not for me! Surely I won't feel this way for five to seven years!"

I wanted to get it over with quickly, and knew I could. I wanted to be happy *NOW!* Well, guess what? He was right. It took much longer than I thought.

I should have listened to the words of Marie Ranier Rilke:

"Be patient toward all that is unsolved in your heart and try to love the questions themselves, like locked rooms and like books that are now written in a very foreign tongue. Do not now seek the answers, which cannot be given you because you would not be able to live them. And the point is, to live everything. Live the questions now. Perhaps you will then gradually, without noticing it, live along some distant day into the answer"

Our Impatient World

In speaking to businesspeople and helping them develop communication teams at work, they told me this: **The generation of "me" people who grew up with the instant gratification mentality are the biggest personnel challenge.** They are used to instant messaging and cell phones connecting them instantly with the real world. They can get instant answers to any questions, not by thumbing laboriously through the card catalog at the library and plowing through shelves of books, but by searching for them on the Internet. High-speed connections give instant access to vast amounts of information. They can buy something on-line in a moment and charge anything quickly and efficiently. They grew up in a society of abundance and prosperity, and are used to it. It translates into their jobs, when they want to advance, make more money, and skip the steps needed to learn what they have to learn and pay their dues. They want it NOW! And because everyone else has this mentality, if you're not running with the pack, you're left behind.

Companies follow that mindset, too. **To boost the bottom line and compete in the marketplace, they want instant results.** The push creates stress. Productivity and business relationships suffer. In an effort to rush results, people are over-worked, competition intensifies, communication breaks down, and the team falls apart. The spiral continues.

Individuals feel the stress. They bring it home. The family feels the strain. They lose balance. All this is the result of striving for quick results when thorough and well-thought-out results work better. All this is a result of striving so fast to increase the bottom line that we lose our people in the shuffle. **Increased job satisfaction, a more productive work environment, happier employees and company stability occur when you take one step at a time.**

First Steps

"Whatever you can do, or dream, you can, so BEGIN IT. Boldness has genius, power and magic in it."— **Goethe**

I took a corporate group on a ropes course teambuilding experience. The goal was to climb the 30-foot tower while attached by ropes and cables to others on the team, then walk along a tight rope to another 30-foot tower. The challenge was to support each other physically and emotionally ... and they did that well. The first one to attempt the step-by-step laborious walk across the rope fell the first time and found himself dangling by the ropes held by his team. He tried again and was successful. Afterwards, he said: **"The first step was intense ... but after that the view was amazing."**

Every January 1, we start out with a new view of life when the ball drops in New York's Times Square. This is the time to start new things: a smoke-free life, a fat-free diet, and new relationships. We ponder for weeks about what we will do new and different in the New Year. New Year's Eve is the first step, as is every month, every day, and every minute. **The challenge is to be present enough to notice these first moments as they come**, put them behind us, and then experience another first moment.

Appreciating the Moments

I like to think of each of our lives as a long adventure novel. Each challenge is a chapter filled with ups and downs, darkness and light, leading to a brilliant conclusion. Each day is a new start, ending in a peaceful night. Each night is a fertile resting place in between. Each person who enters the story is an important character who affects the final outcome, if only in a small way. Most important, **each moment contributes to the next to make the story complete.**

We've all experienced those special peak moments that replay in our heads over and over, when our emotions are intense and focused: when a baby is born, the big promotion comes, or you have a car accident. You feel these moments in your head and your body, and the emotion almost takes your breath away. They can be positive or negative, and they affect you for the rest of your life.

In these intense moments, we are living authentically. We feel the emotion in our heart with true feelings of joy, pain, and sorrow. They come directly from the heart and reflect who we really are and what we value. Our head honors those feelings and translates them into context. Harmony occurs when our heart and our head are on the same page.

If we live day-to-day, step-by-step, and appreciate the moments, we are living each day fully. If you live each day as if it were your last, your view would be so much different. Every moment would be meaningful and special. Every moment would be purposeful. Climbing one step at a time, we appreciate the moments and live this way.

Listen with Your Heart

Appreciating the moments is living in the present. We feel before we think. The heart knows things the head cannot. It speaks what it feels, without judgment. **The moments show us where the feelings, which come from the heart inside of us, join the nature outside of us.** To appreciate the moments is to listen with the heart.

Listen with Your Body

In our world, we buzz around in a fast-moving car. The faster we go, the faster we lose our sense of natural rhythm. We are moving so fast that sometimes we can't even see what we are passing. Our senses are deadened and we have given up the right to enjoy the unencumbered beauty of what is around us. We don't even notice the noise after a while. Those are not peak moments or even memorable moments because speed has erected a barrier that closes us off. Standing on top of a mountain, we actually hear the slow tick tock of the planet. We can listen to the water, wind, and pulse. Sunsets, sunrises, water running, birds chirping, and flowers blooming remind us to slow down and live for the moments. **The moments open up our senses and help us to listen with our bodies.**

Concentrate on the Now

Sometimes we postpone the present by banking on and concentrating on the past and future. We worry about things that are yet to happen ... and things that may never happen. About possible missed opportunities, possible missed achievements we could have made ... and things we didn't get.

By living in the now, we can:

◈ **Enjoy life;**
◈ **Buckle down and get things done;**
◈ **Get through the tough times with less stress;**
◈ **Avoid regret;**
◈ **Do a little at a time;**
◈ **Carry a small load;**
◈ **Feel our emotions.**

A Best Friend - Indeed

Animals show us how to live in the moment. It would be great if our lives were so uncomplicated. By living in the moment, we find happiness through simplicity. Here are some lessons of simplicity you can learn from a dog:

1. Allow the experience of fresh air and the wind in your face to be pure ecstasy.
2. Never pass up an opportunity to go on a joyride.
3. When loved ones come home, always run to greet them.
4. Let others know when they've invaded your territory.
5. Never pretend you're something you're not.
6. When it's in your best interest, practice obedience.
7. Take naps and stretch before rising.
8. Run, romp and play daily.
9. Stop when you have had enough.
10. Be loyal.
11. If what you want lies buried, dig until you find it.
12. When someone is having a bad day, be silent, sit close by and nuzzle him or her gently.
13. Avoid biting when a simple growl will do.
14. On hot days, drink lots of water and lie under a shady tree.

15.On warm days, lie on your back in the grass.
16.When you're happy, dance around and wag your entire body.
17.No matter how often you're scolded, don't buy into the guilt thing and pout ... run right back and make friends.
18.Delight in the simple joy of a long walk.
19.FINALLY... never trust anyone until you sniff their butt.

— **Author Unknown**

Pace and Persistence

"Nothing in the world can take the place of persistence ... TALENT will not: nothing is more common than unsuccessful people with talent
GENIUS will not: unrewarded genius is almost a proverb
EDUCATION will not: The world is full of educated derelicts
PERSISTENCE AND DETERMINATION ALONE ARE OMNIPOTENT"   — **Theodore Roosevelt**

While climbing to the base camp of Mt. Everest, I used a walking stick to help me set a rhythm. As I walked, I would swing the stick forward, plant it with a "tick" noise on a rock in front of me, then take two-steps, and swing it forward again. Soon, I had a rhythm and a sound that coordinated with my deep breathing. Swing, tick, swing, tick. A breath of fresh air in through the nose with the swing ... held with the tick ... and finally out through the mouth. Again and again I did it, until before I knew it, I had enough energy for each step. I was focused, strong, and getting there, little by little, one step at a time. **My body and my mind were in sync.**

Most important, I had to be persistent. Stopping along the trail meant breaking the rhythm and focus, making it harder to get going again. The task was much easier because of the steadiness of the pace. **My senses were awake because of the body and mind rhythm.** I could hear any small animal noise along the way, the yak bells tinkling up the trail, the waterfall just ahead, and the erratic sound of the wind as it blew around the peaks and valleys. All this coordinated with the tick of the stick and my breath going in and out. What I missed in visual stimulation, I got through other sharpened senses.

Twelve people were in our group. Three of us were over 50 years young. The rest were in their 30s. I was in among the elders. We were "the plodders." The young people were "the chargers." They started the first day hiking at a break-neck pace. They pushed hard and moved fast and efficiently but did not acclimate to the altitude on the way. When we plodders arrived at camp, we found the nine chargers flat on their backs, exhausted, and sick from the altitude. We plodded our way there, and were tired but *not* exhausted. We had a great dinner, got up rested after a full night's sleep, and did it again. So did they. With persistence, we all got to the peak. The plodders got there more slowly. We all saw the top of the mountain, but the plodders got to see a lot more along the way.

Charging along through life fast and furiously is a tough way to travel. It's much harder to sustain that pace, and the stopping and starting you need to do is so much harder than plodding along at a steady pace. So it is with the process of transition ... slow and steady wins the race, as the tortoise showed the hare. Keep it up, don't stop, and take one step at a time. **Persistence pays off.**

Commitment

"Until one is committed there is hesitance, the chance to draw back: always ineffectiveness. Concerning all acts of initiative, there is one elementary truth, the ignorance of which kills countless ideas and plans: that the moment one definitely commits oneself, then providence moves too. All sorts of things occur to help one that would never otherwise have occurred. A whole stream of events issues from the decision, raising in one's favor all manner of unforeseen incidents and meetings and material assistance, which no man could have dreamt would have come his way" — **Goethe**

Climbing your mountain will become a reality if you put together your vision, your determination, and your persistence and make a commitment or a **promise** to yourself.

FIRST... promise to get out of bed every day and get moving. Promise to take care of yourself.

NEXT ... promise to take small steps, one after the other ... day by day.

NEXT ... promise to find what you want to do with your life and look for a vision.

NEXT ... commit yourself to taking each step to the peak.

The vision tells you where you are going and what your dream actually looks like. It paints you a mental picture of where you will go. You realize your vision **IF** you are determined, **IF** you are persistent, and **IF** you are committed. **Your vision tells you what you want!**

◆**Determination** is the intensity of willpower you bring to your vision. It is the resolve or fortitude you bring to your challenge. **Your determination tells you how much you want it!**

◆**Persistence** is about how willing you are to persevere. When it gets hard to move on, will you stick it out, be diligent, and keep going, one step at a time? **Your persistence tells you what you will do to get it!**

◆**Commitment** is the pledge you make to realize your dream. It's the promise and assurance that you will do it. **Your commitment tells you that you will promise to do it!**

Vision + Determination + Persistence + Commitment = Conquering Your Mountain

Thomas Edison showed us all of these qualities. He did not graduate from high school. He was not an engineer and not a scientist, yet he knew he could capture light in his bulb shaped object. **He was determined to make it work and kept trying until he finally did.** What made him so committed to his vision? Edison thought of his creative ideas while he was asleep and dreaming. So he took frequent catnaps with a rock in his hand. When he went into a deep sleep, the rock would fall out of his hand and land loudly on the floor below, waking him up, often in the middle of an informative dream. Then he was able to go to his studio and capture the idea on paper. His whole body was committed to his vision.

After trying over 4,000 different materials for his light filament, someone asked him, "Why do you keep trying? Why don't you just give up? It's a stupid idea. Why have you done all this work with no results?"

His response was, "I do have results. I have found 4,000 things that don't work! It will work." And, of course, eventually it did.

Louis L'Amour wrote 350 books before he found a publisher to represent him. The book *The Wizard of Oz* was shopped to over 80 publishers, all of whom rejected it, so the author finally self-published it. Michelangelo broke 400 noses on his statue of David because the marble he was using was not just right. He finally sculpted the David by finding the perfect piece of marble, and then he chipped away all the marble that was not David.

They all had a vision, were determined, persisted, and were strongly committed.

Patience

Just as a fine wine needs time to age and mature, we need time to let the process of transformation happen from the inside out. Just at the time of our lives when we want to move ahead, moving ahead becomes nearly impossible. Just when we are struggling to regain control of our lives, we have no choice but to give up control. We want to move forward one step at a time. Instead we find that we have to take two steps back before we take one more step. All growth is about shedding the old in order to grow the new. Both of these processes take time and patience. **We need patience to marinate and allow the transformation to happen.**

The hermit crab is one animal that is often in transitions. As the crab grows, he becomes too big for his home, so he must find another one that fits him perfectly. He does this many times until he is full-grown. The most vulnerable time for the crab is when he is between the old shell and the new, because he is naked and unprotected. Transition is that vulnerable time for us. As uncomfortable as it is, we *will* find our new home if we move slowly and carefully.

When we feel unprotected and vulnerable, we are open to the world around us. Anyone who has gone through major grief and change will tell you that your whole perspective changes. Things that were so important to us before, no longer matter. All those little things that we didn't notice before are very visible. Like the hermit crab, we slowly crawl to a new home but try to move fast enough to avoid danger. Like the crab, being out of our shell allows us to see new things and a world of possibilities that we never knew existed before.

Survival Tips

❖**Allow yourself to just be.** Being is all about relaxing. To appreciate each step on your path takes presence. Take a deep breath and relax ... pay attention to what is going on around you ... people, things and nature as it is right now. Notice how your body parts feel ... where your legs and arms are ... how your neck muscles feel. Let it all go and open up your senses.

❖**Appreciate the moments.** Think of all those amazing snippets of life that are happening to you, both good and bad. Think in terms of taking it one step at a time. Notice how far you have come.

❖**Listen.** Chart the sounds you hear around you either on paper or mentally. It will help you become more aware of your new surroundings. Listen for the small things.

❖**Practice mindfulness.** Dedicate time to think about the moments of the day. Analyze where your mind and body is in those moments.

❖**Pace yourself.** Slow yourself down. Remember, slow and steady wins the race. How do you slow yourself down? Take breaks, breathe, read a book, take a walk ... whatever makes you take a mind break. During the grief process, I found exercise to be a real vehicle in changing pace. After strenuous exercise, nothing feels better than the shower afterwards. A short walk will do the same thing. The exhale you feel after a change of pace gives you balance and helps you feel better.

❖**Chunk.** Make a list of all the things that challenge you now – ALL of them. Then prioritize them, chunk them into categories, and put them into little invisible boxes that you put on the shelf. Then, starting with box number one, take it down and handle it. Don't even think of the other boxes. You can take them down later. Soon, you'll notice the progress as your shelf empties.

❖**Do small projects.** Take on some small, relaxing projects that have nothing to do with your transition: creative projects such as woodworking or sewing, listen to or play music, art projects, gardening. Put yourself into them totally. Appreciate the moments while you do them.

❖**Connect with nature.** Nature shows us that we are part of a larger whole. Taking a walk, standing by the lake, or looking at a tree helps you feel a peaceful silence. You will feel more alive.

Chapter Nine

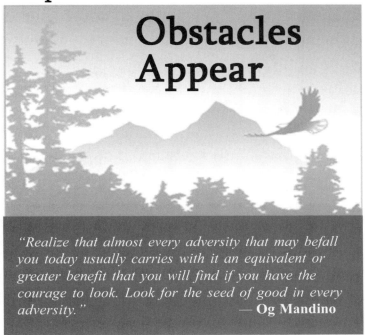

Obstacles Appear

"Realize that almost every adversity that may befall you today usually carries with it an equivalent or greater benefit that you will find if you have the courage to look. Look for the seed of good in every adversity."
— **Og Mandino**

As you travel down the road of life, one thing for sure: **Obstacles will be thrown into your path. No doubt about it.** As if to keep you on your toes and add a little variety to your life, the landscape you are traveling through will be filled with them. Just as you are on the mountain, you can sometimes anticipate your challenges. Sometimes they are self-imposed, and sometimes they come from forces out of your control. Just when you have life all figured out, you find out you're wrong. Something drops into the picture to make you think again.

No matter how big the challenges really are, when you are going through them, they are huge. When we think of major loss, we think of loss of a job, death of a loved one, divorce, or serious illness. But the day-to-day grind of managing teenagers who challenge you with feats of independence, nagging money problems, or relationship difficulties at home or at work are just

When the Obstacle Is You

We all have that inner critic inside our heads. He or she tells us how to feel and how to behave. The inner critic judges us from the inside and tells us what we can't do and how incompetent we are. When we hit the obstacle in our way, the critic tells us to quit. "Don't face it. Don't negotiate it! Don't deal with it. It's too hard for you!" And our progress stops. When we listen, we are pushed into actions we don't mean in spite of the consequences. That inner critic becomes our obstacle.

The critic causes us to make decisions we regret: taking the next drink, hurting someone else, climbing a mountain we aren't qualified to climb. All of these are first steps on a road to self-destruction.

How do we stop the critic from throwing roadblocks on our path? It's just like climbing a mountain.

◈Recognize the peak far in the distance; where you want to go.

◈Lighten your load; use the past as a learning experience.

◈Take one step at a time; concentrate on the present.

When you are on a diet, the cake sitting on your counter may tempt you. You may say, "Okay, maybe I'll just have a small piece on my way through the kitchen. *Only one!*" You do it again the next time you pass through because it really tasted good, and you would hate to see it go to waste. After all, it may be the last piece of cake you ever see. Before you know it, you have eaten five pieces and your pants feel tight. You get discouraged and berate yourself because you are now on a binge. You say to yourself, "Okay, I've blown it. Now I look fat and it's so much work to lose it again! I love eating and I don't care." Instead, own up to what you did, give yourself permission not to be perfect, and say, "Okay, I ate too much today. Now I'll start back to eating the way I want to ... healthy!" Then, let it go. You can change your habits one step at a time.

Our emotions cause us to get in our own way. They affect our behavior and our ability to function. They drive us to swim against the current or lash out at others without thinking. They are our biggest enemies and our closest friends. **Our emotions can become our own self-imposed obstacles.** For example:

◈ Anger that flares up from deep inside can cause us to act without thinking and lash out against others.

◈ Hate can make us act violently without regard for human life.

◈ Joy can cause us to serve others.

◈ Love can cause us to make others love in return.

◈ Loneliness can lead us to do things we don't mean out of desperation.

◈ Emotional trauma can cause strained relationships and physical problems.

◈ Disorientation can cause us to wander aimlessly.

◈ Fear can cause us to be paralyzed.

◈ Despair can cause us to lose hope.

> *"When one door closes, another opens, but we often look so long and so regretfully at the closed door that we don't see the one that has opened for us."*
> **— Alexander Graham Bell**

Managing Obstacles

How we perceive our obstacles determines how we react to them. People can have the same obstacles and challenges, yet perceive them differently. That perception comes from our personality, how we grew up, and the experiences we've had. My three boys are totally different in personality. A challenge to one may not be a challenge to another. Their reactions to the same things are totally different. I may act the same with all of them, and yet they each see me differently.

If my three boys were climbing a mountain, and a sudden a storm approached, my cautious child would want to retreat immediately; my analytical child would think it out, analyze it, and devise a plan; and my adventurous son would say "go for it" no matter what. The perception of the situation is as real for them as the situation itself. **How they react to that perception is a personal choice they make.**

When obstacles appear, we can:

◈**Handle them as they come up ... deal with them, and move on.** Some obstacles are bigger than others, but the more we learn how to negotiate them, the better we get at it. I remember when, as a child, I had to go through a series of allergy shots. The first one was painful and I dreaded the ones to come. The next few were just as bad. But as time went on, they got easier and easier. I knew I couldn't avoid them, so I adjusted. I'm not sure whether they got easier or I got harder.

◈**We can avoid them and retreat.** When I was eight years old, I had a dental trauma and became totally terrified to go to the dentist. Even having my teeth cleaned was frightening. So it's no surprise that as soon as I was old enough to drive, and my mom made an appointment for me, I would simply drive around for an hour and not go. My parents got the bill for the cleanings even if I wasn't there, so I got away with it ... until I got a few huge cavities and *really* had to go to the dentist. Eventually my parents found out. I paid the consequences in several ways: I had painful cavities that needed filling *and* I had to pay my parents back for the appointments I had missed.

How we handle those obstacles in our way is a choice we make. We can overcome them if we handle them with:

- Positive attitude
- Patience
- Perspective
- Flexibility
- Vision

Handle with a Positive Attitude

Sometimes we feel like the mythical character Sisyphus who was punished by the gods and condemned to roll a huge boulder to the top of the mountain for eternity. Just as the rock would get near the top of the mountain, the weight of it would be too great and it would roll back down on the straining body of Sisyphus. Like Sisyphus, we have those everyday nagging obstacles that we handle with all of our strength ... all the time. The rock is always there and we strain against it, trying to make headway, only to end up exactly where we started, seeing no progress in our relentless struggle.

My friend Casey has a disabled child. Every day she deals with the struggle of pushing the rock up the hill, and every day she feels like she ends up just where she started. Her child's situation will not change. How does she handle it? With a smile on her face, seeing the joyful part of her struggle in the occasional smile on the face of her child.

The test is not the distance we push the rock or the progress we make. It is not the speed with which we push it. It is *how* we push the rock. We are defined by those moments when we are pinned under the rock: that nagging burden we might be stuck with ... illness, daily responsibilities. Will we complain, blame, and harbor resentment? Or will we push those rocks with dignity and a smile on our face?

Handle with Patience

Then there are the leeches. I'd heard about them before traveling to Nepal but had no idea what they were really like. In the early fall monsoon season, leeches are everywhere. They're on the leaves and branches of bushes and trees, just waiting to drop down on you as you pass below. We protected ourselves with high boots and pants that hugged our ankles. We wore long sleeved shirts with tight fitting cuffs and collars, and hats that dropped over our necks and ears. Still, the leeches, which were in search of warm blood, got through to our skin. They found their way to our warmest, moistest body parts. They even screwed themselves out of the mud and into the bottom of our shoes. They don't hurt... they are not a medical problem. At the end of each day, we'd throw our clothes off and burn the leeches off or pour salt water on them, which made them shrivel and die.

Think about the leeches in your life: bosses, paperwork, traffic jams, taxes, road construction, things and people that sap you of your energy and your life's blood. Will you let them suck away and cause you to lose focus on where you are going? Or will you adjust to them, patiently, and put them in their proper place at the end of the day?

Handle with Perspective

I went kayaking for a month in Prince William Sound, Alaska with a wilderness leadership group. Mosquitoes were a huge problem. They swarmed all over us, bugged us, and stung us. They were in our ears, in our eyes, in our food, and in our sleeping bags. The only relief was out on the water in our kayaks. We also found that if we sat on the beach with an umbrella over our heads, they would not go under it and bother our heads. So we learned to stay away from them as best we could, and adjust to those times when we had no choice.

Some obstacles we cannot control. There's nothing wrong with avoiding negative things if we can, but we can't avoid some of those "pesty" nagging challenges. Are they going to control us or are we going to do whatever we can to control them? Are we going to waste energy on things we can't change, or put them in proper perspective and look at them as small pesty annoyances?

Handle with Flexibility

Our family went on a rafting adventure on the Pecare River in Costa Rica. A young and reckless Costa Rican boatman was in the raft with my family of four. The first part of the river was quiet, serene, and beautiful as it meandered in the dense jungle. As I dangled my hand into the calm warm water, I noticed a fairly decent wake trailing from my finger—evidence of the river's strong undercurrent. I thought about the force of the Gulf Stream that governs our whole weather system—a strong and awesome force. I was soon to find out that the river was in control ... not me.

Suddenly, I was flying through the air, hitting my face with the paddle. I was thrown, bleeding, into the churning river.

Quickly and efficiently, my boat mates grabbed my life vest and yanked me back into the raft. Five minutes later, we went over another small waterfall. The awesome force of the water threw my eldest son out of the raft and slammed it against a boulder, trapping him underneath. For what seemed like an eternity, he was trapped. Suddenly he popped up, gasping for breath … and terrified. He had to relax and let the water spit him out. By letting go of control, he found himself again.

Isn't that just the way life is? Sometimes those unseen forces can hit us when we least expect it. They are strong enough to throw us for a loop, pull us down, and leave us swirling out of control. If we give up control and relax, sometimes we just pop up into the light again. We can't fight the demon that is too strong for us; we waste energy and tire. If we remain loose and flexible, we can adjust long enough to let the negative force pass us by.

I always marvel at the sight of the single tree growing out of a crack in a rock on a mountainside. What makes that tree grow with such limited resources while others perish?

Trees that are crowded together take advantage of unlimited resources. They grow easily, but are weak and susceptible to disease. On the other hand, those that struggle to reach the light of the sun, or push hard to find the minerals in the soil, become flexible and adaptable. They have tighter growth rings, become strong, and more flexible. **Struggling with obstacles along our path forces us to be flexible and stronger.**

Handle with Vision

The river follows its natural course. It twists and turns as it makes its way around boulders and through canyons. Sometimes it goes over the obstacles in its path, but usually it adjusts by changing direction. The obstacles themselves are changed by the force and power of the river and are gradually smoothed, polished, and cut away.

Traveling the river of life, we have similar obstacles in our way. If we aren't awake and alert, we may run right into them … and then have to struggle hard to extricate ourselves. If we were like the river, we could anticipate them and change directions. We could use our force to change them, too.

Kayaking taught me a lot about handling obstacles in my way. I learned one of my greatest kayaking tricks from the art of fly-fishing. I found that if I wore polarized sunglasses, I could actually see the fish under water, dangle the fly over their heads, and wait for them to strike. I wear them when I kayak, too, so I can see the rocks below the surface. In anticipation of the rock ahead, I can adjust my position and turn before I hit it. That way, I avoid hitting it and losing control.

At the same time, if my vision is focused *too* far ahead, I may just miss the very rock right under my nose. **Vision must be intense and focused and at the same time be able to see the whole picture.**

Wouldn't it be great if we could avoid all the obstacles by simply turning before we get to them? The fact is, we can't always see what's coming our way. **But if we are awake and alert, we may be able to handle them with more vision and insight. If we are prepared, physically and mentally, we may be able to be strong enough to turn before we hit them. If we can see them coming, we may be able to avoid them entirely.**

Between the Rock and the Hard Place
When we are stuck between the rock and the hard place, trapped with nowhere to go, we face the impasse. This is the place where progress halts. We are deadlocked and stuck. We can't see the next step because there is no next step. We have run out of gas. The obstacle is so high that we can't get over, under, around, or through it.

When mountain climbing, we get up in the dark and make our your ascent before the weather changes; winds are calmer in the morning and the storm clouds that almost always gather by mid-day have not yet arrived. Still, the wind can suddenly change when we are not expecting it, making the conditions treacherous. This is when we face the impasse and we must decide what to do next.

Being at the impasse is emotionally and physically stressful. We can become paralyzed and stuck there. Usually, we rescue ourselves when our neurons react to the stress by firing at break-neck speed. The result can be peak performance and mental clarity. Remarkable solutions to impossible problems can occur in these moments. If we practice approaching them deliberately and clearly, we get through those tough times more easily.

How do we handle the impasse?

◈**Step back and take another look.** Take a deep breath and get good cleansing oxygen into your body so you can think clearly. Be objective and look for possibilities. Think about what you may have missed. Think about changing your perspective. Make sure to weigh the consequences of whatever action you take. Most important, listen to your heart and your intuition will tell you the right thing to do.

◈**Search for the familiar.** Look for what experience has taught you about what works and what doesn't work. Think about what you are normally comfortable doing. Take the information you know and factor it into what you don't know. Try to think clearly.

◈**Ask for help if you can.** If others are present, work together to pool your resources. If you are alone, ask God or a spiritual presence to help you.

◈**Take your best educated guess.** Factor all you have done so far and make a decision regarding what your plan of action will be.

◈**Move slowly and deliberately.** Move cautiously. Be awake and alert every step of the way. Be clearheaded and analytical. If you need to, you can stop and go through the analysis again.

You Have Four Simple Choices:

#1-Stay where you are until things change

Sometimes the smartest thing to do when the weather changes is take cover and wait, especially when the conditions are not in your control.

Sitting on the Glacier

My friend Susie went with a group to climb Mt. Rainier near Seattle, Washington. She was prepared from the inside – the adventure attitude was hers and she knew she was mentally ready to take on the challenge. She'd worked hard on the treadmill to be in good physical shape. About three weeks before the climb, she went to Colorado and took a long hike with her backpack and brand new glacier boots (glacier boots are hard plastic boots like ski boots that are stiff and non-breathable). In breaking the boots in, she ended up with blisters on her feet that stopped her from doing any more practice runs before going to Washington.

Her expedition was divided into four climbing groups. She was one of two females, and at 58 years young, was 30 years older than the other woman. The first day was "climbing school" where skills were reinforced and tested. The next day they hiked to the base camp about six hours away. She was tired, but did well. That night, she went to bed early and woke up at midnight for the ascent.

Her group was roped together and started hiking. It didn't take long for her to realize she was having trouble breathing and keeping up. She was tired from climbing school. She was used to walking at her own pace, pausing occasionally to take an extra breath. But roped together with others, she had to travel the same steady, yet strong, pace the others set. She could never stop to catch her breath and was being pushed too fast. She labored for the first hour and a half, and then they stopped for a short time. They hiked for another hour, and stopped again.

By now, she was in serious trouble. This was her point of impasse. She knew she had to stop right there or jeopardize the safety of the whole group. Knowing what she knew about the wilderness, Susie opted to stay where she was. Taking an extra sleeping bag and flares, she made herself comfortable, bundled in lots of warm clothes, and sat on the glacier for about six hours, when the rest of the group returned from their ascent.

Susie assessed her situation and herself. She realized her own limits and her responsibility to her team. She did the right thing and saved herself and the team.

#2-Change Direction and Change the View

When you have a rock in your way, you can't see over it or around it. This is a time for creative thinking and personal adjustment. Changing direction means thinking it through and figuring out another way. If you are plodding along on the trail, and it narrows to a rock ledge, you may have to do some creative rope climbing to get around it. If you are facing a difficult job market and can't find any way to get a job where you can use your skills, you may have to make a personal adjustment to think of another facet of the job market that you can jump into.

Another Lesson from the Eagle

The eagle knows when a storm is approaching long before it breaks. He will fly to a high spot and wait for the winds to come. When the storm hits, he sets his wings so the wind will pick him up and lift him above the storm. While the storm rages below, the eagle is soaring above it. The eagle does not escape the storm. He simply uses the winds to lift him higher. He rises on the winds that bring the storm and views it from a different perspective. When the storms of life come upon us, and we experience sickness, tragedy, failure and disappointment, we do not have to overcome them. We can use their power to rise above and look at them differently.

#3-Forge Ahead and Get Through It

When things get tough, it's okay to face the challenge head on and take the consequences as they come. After analyzing the situation, we may find it is the only choice.

The Sherpa on the Bridge

One very windy day in Nepal, I approached a beautiful bridge built over a raging gorge. The bridge was a typical Nepalese bridge, attached on either end by a few poles, held together with small planks and ropes. There were many of them in Nepal and they were frighteningly unstable. They would swing, lurch, and groan as you walked across. I always *knew* I would end up falling and crashing to the rocks below.

One particular bridge was missing many of its planks. When I got to the beginning of it, I stood debating whether or not I should cross. Should I go back and find another path? Was there even another path? After standing there for what seemed like forever, a small Sherpa woman showed up carrying a large basket filled with pots and pans. She was about four feet tall and had no shoes. Her clothes were tattered, and she was missing teeth in the front. She turned to me and looked straight into my eyes. With a big smile on her face, she put her hands together in prayer position, bowed, and said, "Namaste." Then she turned around, and without delay, walked right across the bridge.

Okay, I get it. It must be safe. So I stepped back, rejuvenated myself, found a focus point, and with Sherpa-type confidence I walked across the bridge.

An Act of Bravery

Aron Ralston was an expert mountain climber. In early summer 2003, he embarked on a solo rock climbing expedition in Canyonlands National Park, Utah. He was maneuvering around a narrow slot canyon three feet wide. When he put his hand on the side of a boulder, it shifted two to three feet, pinning his hand and trapping him. He tried freeing himself with ropes, anchors, and anything he was able to reach in his backpack. He was stuck at the impasse. His repeated efforts failed. Before long, he ran out of water and food, so there he remained, for five days.

Aron knew he had no choice. To save himself, he would have to cut off his hand. The pocketknife he had in his pocket was dull, but he managed to cut off his lower arm and hand. He then rappelled 75 feet to the canyon floor. He hiked five miles with his arm in a makeshift sling fashioned out of his dried up camelback water carrier. Rescue workers said they had never seen anybody who had this much tenacity and will to live.

They're used to seeing disoriented climbers who lose their way or just give up while waiting for help. Aron forged ahead, and got through it.

#4-Climb Down

Sometimes you have to give up and retreat from your position. If you come across a rock ledge you can't get around, over, or through, you may have to give up and climb back down. You may not find a place to attach the rope that will help you skirt the obstacle.

Or, if bad weather surprises you and you have time to avoid a dangerous situation, retreat may be the smart thing to do. At least you will live to climb another day. If you want something that you just can't get, if your goals are unrealistic or the resources are not available for you to achieve your goals, then you may have to give them up. Trying something new is not defeat; it's a temporary re-direction.

My friend Sue was married for 19 years. Her husband was a nice man and a good provider, but had a drinking problem that got worse over the years. She decided to "hang in" with him and help him with his problem. She covered up for him in public, and eventually ignored and denied the problem. She kept hoping he would get help, the problem would go away, and he would recover. She tried going to Al-Anon groups to get help, but her marriage got more and more lonely. His behavior became erratic and dangerous. One night he arrived home late after drinking ... and beat her.

Sue finally arrived at her impasse. Her situation was bad and she had to make a decision: Should she stay in the marriage and tolerate the hopeless situation of loneliness and abuse? Or should she climb down and get out of the marriage? Both options were frightening to her. Sue listened to her support group, her intuition, her heart, and her head. Ultimately, she left him. She got the divorce and did what she felt was right and healthy for herself and her family.

One thing is universally true: Every problem comes with a gift in its hand.

Be it strength, clarity of vision, newfound talents, new appreciation, or new perspective, you will find that the obstacles in your life will make you stronger and better. If you are open-minded, do your best, and find the lessons in the problem, then you will find great wisdom. The obstacles become the greatest gifts.

"Our greatest glory consists not in never falling, but in rising every time we fall."— **Ralph Waldo Emerson**

Survival Tips

◈**Silence the inner critic.** Whenever you resort to negative self-talk, think about that inner critic sitting on your shoulder. Give him a face and slap him around. You might even draw him on a piece of paper and throw it right in the garbage. It sounds ridiculous, I know, but you will get a thrill out of getting rid of him, once and for all.

◈**Keep an anger journal.** If you are prone to anger, list all the things that make you angry on a daily basis ... people, road rage, situations you might encounter every day. Be careful not to make your obstacles yourself. Can you think of another way to deal with it? Analyze what sets you off, and avoid those situations any way you can.

◈**Concentrate on your positive emotional moments.** Journal about them and remind yourself what they felt like and how they affected your behavior. Positive begets positive. Try to reframe your obstacles into opportunities for adventure and positive change.

◈**Make a timeline.** Make a list of the obstacles you've had to handle that you remember. If you are dealing with job loss, list all the tough situations at work you can recall. When you were most successful, how did you do it? How could you build on that next time around? If you are dealing with loss, what did you learn from past losses that can help you now? You'll be amazed at all the things you have survived. You'll discover that you are already an expert at survival.

◈**List the past roadblocks you have handled.** Could you have handled them differently in terms of positive attitude, patience, perspective, flexibility, and vision?

❖**How controllable are the obstacles in your life?** Can you change them by your own actions? If so, make a plan:

- Step back and analyze them.
- Search for the familiar.
- Ask for help.
- Make an educated plan of attack.
- Move ahead slowly and deliberately.
- Are they out of your control? Are you helpless to alter them?

If so:

- Lighten your load!
- Give up control, so you can move on with your life.

❖**Identify daily obstacles.** What are the daily obstacles in your way? Think of them objectively. What can you do to handle them now?

- Stay where you are and wait for things to change.
- Change direction and take another route.
- Forge ahead and face the challenges head on.
- Retreat and move away from them.

Chapter Ten

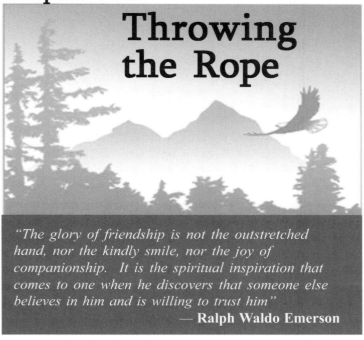

Throwing the Rope

"The glory of friendship is not the outstretched hand, nor the kindly smile, nor the joy of companionship. It is the spiritual inspiration that comes to one when he discovers that someone else believes in him and is willing to trust him"
— **Ralph Waldo Emerson**

Climbing mountains and going through transition teaches us how much we need each other to survive. When life gets hard, the burdens are lighter and easier to carry when we have physical and emotional support.

Connecting With Our Team

A climbing team consists of unique individuals, each performing an important role in the expedition's success. We have one person responsible for logistics, an expert climbing technician, a person responsible for food procurement, and the communication expert. Each team member is chosen with great care. In addition to his or her specific role, each person must value and respect the others and put the team's needs above his or her own.

When the trail is tough and conditions make hiking difficult, team members are attached to each other with a rope. **The rope holds them together and becomes the common bond that ensures they go in the same direction safely.**

❖At the front of the rope line is the **team leader.**

•The team leader sets the pace. If the pace is too slow, the team becomes discouraged. If the pace is too fast, they burn out and get tired. The team leader must give everyone a chance to catch their breath and remain energized. To function efficiently, the team must remain perfectly balanced between burnout and boredom.

•The team leader is the encourager that holds the group together when things get tough. As the encourager, he/she gives emotional support and help when people need it. The team leader usually stops to check in with everyone to make sure they are okay.

•The team leader is the most experienced person on the team and is able to anticipate the obstacles they may encounter. When crossing the glacier, he/she uses a probe to test the terrain for crevices that may be hidden below the crust of snow. The others then follow, knowing the terrain is safe.

❖The people in the back and in the middle are the strongest team members. They have a lot of general knowledge, experience, and physical strength. They are the team workhorses who can be counted on as anchors: strong and steady. They communicate and help everyone along the way, especially the least experienced climbers.

❖The people with the least experience are sandwiched between the others. For the team to work well together, they must learn from the others and be open and receptive. They must succeed if the team is to succeed.

Each individual must be able to depend on the other team members and know they will do their job. To work together, they must go in the same direction, with compatible values, and communicate openly and honestly, no matter what their individual personality differences might be. Just as a car engine, all the parts are necessary for the engine to work. If it is not greased and oiled and cared for, the engine will be sluggish. If one part is weak and doesn't function properly, the engine doesn't run well. If a part is broken, the engine won't run at all.

The rope is not only the thread of life for the climbing team, but it is also the common bond that holds them together. The team goes in the same direction, at the same pace, safely when they are attached to the rope. The weakest people are supported and held up, and the others compensate for them. At work, the team that shares a common purpose and values holds on to the same rope. By traveling and working together, they make progress in achieving their goals.

The rope is also a lifeline to the world outside the team. When they need extra strength and leverage, they can attach the rope to solid rocks. Likewise, in your business and in life, you often need to throw the rope to outside experts: lawyers, accountants, doctors, etc. These people share your common direction, yet they offer another dynamic. They offer their own strength, from the outside. In the grief / change transition period, we find some of our greatest strength comes from outsiders who are able to be objective and yet go the same direction we are going. We may need to throw the rope to encouragers and the problem solvers.

How does the team work together?

- They walk at a pace that works for everyone, even the weakest on the team.
- They check in with each other and communicate openly.
- They care about each other.
- They remain awake and alert for their own safety and that of their team.
- If someone falls while hanging on the rope, everyone knows they must flip over, dig the ice ax into the ice and snow, and create a failsafe to catch the others as they fall.
- They do their job.
- They trust each other.

When I forget that I have a responsibility to do my part in working with my team, be it friends, family, or work teams, I turn to a powerful lesson from nature.

Lessons From Geese

In the fall, geese fly in a V formation as they migrate south for the winter. Here is what science has discovered about why they fly that way:

> ◈**FACT 1:** As each goose flaps its wings, it creates an "uplift" for the birds that follow. By flying in a "V" formation, the whole flock adds 71% greater flying range than if each bird flew alone.

> •**LESSON:** People who are part of a team, sharing a common direction and sense of community, can get where they are going quicker and easier because they travel on the thrust of one another. Individuals who are part of a team should lift each other up along the way

> ◈**FACT 2:** When a goose falls out of formation, it suddenly feels the drag and resistance of flying alone. It quickly moves back into formation to take advantage of the lifting power of the bird immediately in front of it.

> •**LESSON:** If we have as much sense as a goose, we will stay in formation and share information with those headed where we want to go. We accept their help and give our help to others.

> ◈**FACT 3:** When the lead goose tires, it rotates back into the formation and another goose flies to the point position.

> • **LESSON:** It pays to take turns doing the hard tasks and sharing leadership. As with geese, people are interde-

pendent on each other's skills, capabilities, and unique arrangements of gifts, talents, or resources.

◈**FACT 4:** The geese flying in formation honk to encourage those up front to keep up their speed.

- **LESSON:** In groups where there is encouragement, production is much greater. The power of encouragement (to stand by one's heart or core values and encourage the heart and core of others) is the quality we seek. Words of support and inspiration energize those on the front line, helping them to keep pace in spite of the day-to-day pressures and fatigue. It is important that our honking is encouraging **and not just honking.**

◈**FACT 5:** When a goose gets sick, wounded, or shot down, two geese drop out of formation and follow it down to help and protect it. They stay with it until it dies or is able to fly again. Then, they launch out with another formation or catch up with the flock.

- **LESSON:** If we have as much sense as geese, we will stand by each other in difficult times as well as when we are strong. We will stand up for each other, especially when things get rough, and see each other through.

The next time you see a formation of geese, remember what nature has taught us...

"It is a reward, challenge & privilege to be a contributing member of a team."

Appreciating Differences
The challenge of working together as a team is being able to honor individual personality differences. We all have different personalities: introverted or extroverted, fast or slow, glass half empty or glass half full attitude, etc. When we are on a team with people who are different than us, we need

to accept them just the way they are for the team to be efficient. The challenge is to combine our styles with theirs.

For example, I am very outgoing and have a lot of energy. I throw myself "out there" and think about it later. I get along perfectly with others like me, but have to constantly remind myself to slow down with others who are different.

On my expedition to Nepal, I had a tent mate who was very reserved. Every time I asked her questions to get to know her, she would close up. The more I prodded, the less response I got. The less response I got, the more I resented her lack of communication. I found myself judging her on my terms. I thought to myself, "She's a snob. She doesn't like me. She has a negative attitude."

After days of trying to get to know her, I gave up and slowed down around her. Then she started to open up. I finally realized that she was introverted and probably very comfortable with herself. She loved to process experiences internally. As an extrovert, I was trying to move her with the "Mack truck" approach. I came on way too strong for her, and it made her uncomfortable. The minute I backed off and stopped invading her space, she saw me differently. I learned to honor who she was without judgment. Now I look at others differently, too. I learned to be myself and let others be themselves. Being different does not mean being right or wrong … it just means being different.

Together we made a great combination. By being more introverted and more cautious, she was able to see things from a different perspective than I could. She was intelligent and introspective and analyzed situations thoroughly. I was out there, experiencing it all, not missing anything and letting my energy go everywhere. Together, we made a perfect whole.

Nature has many examples of different species that work together for their very survival. Lichens are an example of a symbiotic relationship. They are made up of two "unlikes" that live together and are totally dependent on each other: part algae and part fungus joined together. The algae provide photosynthesis and food for the fungus. The fungus provides shelter for the algae.

They are an important part of our environment. Their tiny root system threads into the rock they sit on, breaking the rock apart as time goes on. The little cracks trap soil. They emit carbon dioxide that, combined with moisture, creates carbonic acid: eroding the limestone whose dust is then given back to the earth. In addition, the lichen is a wonderful food source for moose.

In the process of transition, we need others, ESPECIALLY at that time when we are the most vulnerable. By interacting with those who are different than us, we are able to find the help we need and use other people's experience and perspective to see the world of possibilities.

Asking For Help

Some of us have a hard time asking for support and help, especially when we need it most. Perhaps we fear judgment, don't want to appear weak, or are so used to struggling through tough times alone. Asking for help honors the other person. They are almost always flattered that you considered them able to help. So asking for help makes them feel important and boosts them too. I found when I really needed help and advice, people were always willing to help or find other solutions.

Relationships Change

During the period of grief and change I looked at relationships with others differently. My struggle to find my footing sent me inside myself looking out. I looked at others going about their daily lives while I was suffering inside. In my state, their concern about mundane things seemed ridiculous, and I had little tolerance for complaints about any of the silly day-to-day annoyances. They just didn't seem important. I felt insignificant and jealous. I was so self-absorbed about my own struggles that I had trouble seeing past them. In fact, **I found that those who reached out to me at this time were my life preservers.**

Old friendships were tested during this period. Some of them faded away. It's painful, but it almost always happens. Some people had a hard time understanding and dealing with my loss, so they avoided me. Some were reminded of their own mortality and didn't want to face the reality of it. Some had thought of us as a couple, and couldn't see me as a single. Some couldn't face me because they had unresolved issues of their own. When my friend Joe lost his job, some of his friends seemed embarrassed for him, so they stayed away. They didn't know what to say to him, so they took the easy way out and said nothing.

Alice and Jim were good friends of ours. Our children had grown up together and had even been college roommates. The night Tom died, Alice and Jim arrived at my door so Alice could cry on my shoulder; she was having a hard time dealing with the death of her sister a few months earlier and this was one more loss for her to bear. They were as supportive as they could be but I didn't hear from them again. Five months later, I called Alice. She was friendly as ever. We talked about Tom and how I was doing without him. Then another five months went by. I finally figured out that she couldn't deal with having me in her life because of the pain she was already feeling. She did the best she could.

On the other hand, the transition enhanced some past relationships. The dynamic of the connection changed. Those who went out of their way to be kind and understanding were made even more special by the struggle we went through together. For example, when Joe lost his job, he found amazing support from the people who had been through the same thing. They knew what he was going through so they embraced him.

The new friendships I developed during my transition saved me. People came into my life and viewed me as I am, and not as part of a couple. They helped me identify myself as a single, independent, and capable person. They did it by developing the **heart connection.**

Making the Heart Connection

"Kindness in words ... creates confidence; kindness in thinking ... creates profoundness;kindness in giving ... Creates love.'— **Lao-Tzu**

The heart connection is creating relationships based on honest caring and concern for the other person, not yourself. These are give-and-take connections – you can get what you need and, in turn, they get what they need. It's valuing the other person, no matter how different; it's not making judgments about them based on your own criteria. It's about using positive body language and asking questions to understand them.

Have you ever talked to someone and noticed them looking over your shoulder to see who *else* they could talk to? Have you talked to someone and deep down you knew they weren't listening? Instead, they were thinking about something else, or thinking about what they will say next. How does that make you feel? It makes me feel unappreciated. I feel as if what I'm saying doesn't matter ... as if I don't matter.

Making a heart connection is about caring enough about the other person to really listen to what he or she is saying ... listening with your heart, not just your ears. It's hard to fake true caring. We can "read" insincerity in each other. Caring is about being authentic. Caring is about taking yourself out of it and focusing on the other person. When we are listening with our hearts, we create an authentic relationship. If you do that for others, it comes back to you.

What happens is this:

- The more you care about someone else, the more he or she will care about you.
- The more you honor someone else, the more he or she will honor you.
- The more you listen to someone else, the more he or she will listen to you.

"If you maintain a feeling of compassion, loving kindness, then something automatically opens your inner door. Through that, you can communicate much more easily with other people. And that feeling of warmth creates a kind of openness. You'll find that all human beings are just like you, so you'll be able to relate to them more easily ... creating a spirit of friendship."

— **Dalai Lama**

You make a heart connection by:

◈ Asking questions to learn about the other person;

◈ Not making judgments about others ... and allowing them to be themselves;

◈ Being authentic and letting others know how you feel in a safe and non-threatening way;

◈ Opening your heart and really caring about what others say;

◈ Creating a safe place for others to have honest communication ... without cell phone interruptions and pagers buzzing;

◈ Not fidgeting, but concentrating on the conversation;

◈ Making eye contact ... looking not *at* their eyes but *through* their eyes into their heart, searching for what the other person is really saying, not what the person's voice is saying;

◈ Checking in with others to make sure you understand what they are saying;

◈ Asking questions to clarify and get more information without probing for information.

During the grief process, I worked with children who were suffering with cancer. These children had amazing courage and strength. When I established the heart connection with them ... playing, talking, just being together ... I got back much more than I gave. By sharing their suffering with them, my suffering was diminished. It helped me put my grief in perspective.

In working with companies I have found the same thing over and over again. Communication is not what it should be. Why? Because management often thinks communication is all about:

◈Letting people know how *they* feel and what *they* believe;

◈Talking *to* them (not with them).

When people at work feel they are being talked to and that there is no open and honest two-way communication, they feel devalued. They lose their creativity, enthusiasm, and motivation. They pass information to each other as they stand around the water cooler. Little information comes from the source: management. Critical issues go unsolved and communication gets worse. The spiral has begun:

- Workers feel unappreciated.
- They lose self-esteem.
- They hate their job.
- They become unmotivated.
- Company productivity suffers.
- People quit or are fired.
- The company has to spend money to replace them and train new people.

Taking the time to make the heart connection saves time and money and leads to a happier, more productive work place. **HEART CONNECTIONS at work will make the road easier for those who are facing change.**

Create a Safe Place

All relationships need a safe place to grow and flourish. A safe place is a warm fuzzy blanket where you can sit in your most comfortable pajamas, breathe deeply, and let your stomach hang out. You can laugh and cry, say what you mean, and be yourself.

Whether you're interacting with sales managers, people who are suffering loss, or the checker at the grocery store, a warm open heart, a smile, and a few sincere, friendly words can create a safe place.

In the movie *The Horse Whisperer* with Robert Redford, the horse whisperer develops relationship with horses by creating heart connection.

A mare nurtures her colt by gently nudging it and caring for it. She connects to her colt's soul. The Horse Whisperer develops the soul connection by emulating that relationship: creating a safe, non-threatening place by physically hunching down; making heart-connected eye contact; and standing quietly, waiting for the horse to make the first move. The Horse Whisperer creates a strong solid bond on a soul level by creating an encouraging environment of unconditional acceptance. You can force the horse into submission by bending its will and creating submissive behavior based on fear. This horse *breaking* approach works to make the horse do what *you* want, but it does not create relationship and an unbreakable bond.

It works for us, too. **You can develop a much happier, fulfilled, and motivated workforce by becoming "people whisperers."** In the sales company, the manager does not encourage productivity or help others to live up to their potential by controlling subordinates. He or she does it by creating a comfortable environment so the employees can thrive.

In grief and change, honest communication on a soul level only takes place when we feel unconditional acceptance. Until that bond is created between two people, we feel isolated, unappreciated, and misunderstood. When a person listens with compassion and truly understands, he or she creates a safe place. At the same time, that person honors us and helps lighten our burden of pain.

Find the Rope

Developing a relationship and starting the connection is finding the single thread of commonality that will hold you together. A common bond develops when two people find even a small thing they may share – where they grew up, a favorite movie, a favorite food, anything. Finding that rope of commonality creates the bond that holds you together. How do you find the commonality? **By asking questions...and listening.**

In transition, those relationships built on the common thread boost you into your new life. You experience an instant bond when you have something in common with another. I felt instantly connected to widows and widowers who knew what I was going through and understood my experiences and fears. I found myself connecting with them at a deep level. They were the only ones who could really understand me, and I them. We helped each other get through the ups and downs of the grief process.

Find What They Value

You will learn what other people value by asking questions and listening. Do they think with their body, with their head, or with their heart? Are they energized by stimulation of the body, head, or heart?

◆**BODY** ... Are they physical and athletic? Are sensual experiences important to them, such as art and music? Does the possession of *things* make them happy?

◆**HEAD** ... Do they think with their head? Are they "numbers people" who love details, computers, figuring things out? Do they love to learn?

◆**HEART** ... Are they relationship people? Do they care very much for a cause they may believe in? Do they think with their heart?

Honoring what someone else values and acknowledging what they believe in will help create the heart connection. For example, one of my sons is a high heart person, who is a passionate political activist. He lives and breathes and feels everything that happens in our troubled world. He talks about it constantly... and drives me nuts. It's not necessarily where *my* focus is, but when I feel we are drifting apart, I pick up the paper and find lots of things to ask him about ... things that I, undoubtedly, know nothing about. It may not be something I'm interested in, but it doesn't hurt me to stretch my boundaries and learn something new ... and he loves to talk about it.

What am I doing? I'm letting him know that I value his opinion, which is important for someone who is in transition from boy to man. He is much more open with me if I try to understand what is important to him. The bonus is this… the relationship becomes stronger, and I learn something, too.

Find Out What They Need

Solid relationships are not based on what *you* need, but on what the other person needs. **The best way to honor others is to treat them the way they want to be treated.**

That's easy to say, but what if you want to develop a relationship with someone who is self-serving and only wants it all for him or herself? Do you still treat the person the way he or she wants to be treated? We are all trying to fulfill our needs, and hidden behind what we want is a need that is hungering to be fulfilled. Ask questions to find what is hidden underneath their skin.

Several years ago I ran bike and hiking trips for an adventure travel company: biking through Yellowstone National Park and hiking in the Canadian Rockies. Usually the people I led were great, *but* occasionally I ran into some difficult ones. I remember one couple who found everything they could think of to complain about – the hotel room, the food, the bikes, etc. They wanted special treatment. Finally, I decided that I needed to develop a heart connection with them to find out how I could make them happy. So I sat them down and asked, "If money were no object, and you could have anything you wanted on this trip, what would that be for you?"

They wanted the best room in the hotel with the best view, the best restaurants, and the most beautiful scenery in Montana. I told them that I could give them some of those things, but not all. I told them exactly how the reservations were made, the food was arranged, and the bike route was chosen. I decided after talking to them that they were a couple who was used to being in control. Part of the problem was that I was in control of the trip, not them. I adjusted my behavior and gave them what they needed.

Every day, I talked to them about the route before we started. I explained everything in detail and I let them have some input into organizing the day. I made them feel valued and gave them some control. I gave them what they needed. They became wonderful friends, supportive team members, and great clients. How did I do it? **I asked questions and I listened. I cared. I gave them what they needed.**

Trust

Trust is the invisible knot that holds the rope together. It's the strong bond that can mean the difference between life and death on the mountain. When we say the marriage ceremony is the time when we "tie the knot," we are saying that the two loose ends come together in a commitment to move together in the same direction and create a tight solid circle. **The knot signifies commitment.**

The square knot is one of perfect symmetry: two overhand knots are pulled together equally. If the cross ends of the second knot are wrong, the knot jams and has to be cut. If a bump occurs because of a wrong twist, the knot jiggles loose. The knot has to be tied just right to allow movement, flexibility, and strength. So it is with relationships ... if the parties bond too tight, it strangles them; if too loose, they fall apart.

When the climbers are roped together, trust is the necessary communication vehicle. Often climbers are too far apart and verbal or physical communication is not possible. **Communication is through trust.**

Survival depends on:

Trusting with your heart, and not using muscles or words.

Trusting that when things get tough, you will help each other unselfishly.

Trusting that you are connected by the rope in a heart connection.

Business With Heart

I had a small condominium that I sold "by owner." At the time, I was working with a software company, helping them overcome communication issues. Here I was, working with people to help them build trust with each other, while communicating with my buyer through lawyers and accountants. It sounded a little hypocritical to me. So I decided to have an honest talk with the buyer … to **create a heart connection** and bring that into our business dealings.

We agreed that we could save a lot of time and money if we worked together. We wanted to eliminate hard feelings that could result from using the lawyers. So we agreed to meet at a coffee shop with our unsigned contracts in hand. We would each bring a prioritized list of our financial and personal needs. We agreed that if either one of us felt uncomfortable with the process, it would be okay to get lawyers involved … no questions asked.

So, with double lattes in hand, we spent the first thirty minutes getting to know each other – what our lives were like, what we valued, what we needed. It was clear we needed different things: her priority was the closing date because she had a child in high school who wanted to be in his current house at graduation. That meant I had to get a bridge loan for the time gap. I needed a set amount of money for the down payment … and so did she. I "fessed up" about a furnace problem.

This is what we agreed to: Because her son's last month in high school was the highest consideration, we agreed to close later, on her schedule. In turn, she agreed to pay half of the bridge loan costs. We agreed on a price… somewhere between what both of us wanted. I fixed the furnace. We shared one lawyer. We saved ourselves a lot of aggravation and money.

We used the **heart connection** to create an honest relationship. While it's naïve to think all business can be conducted that way, creating relationships based on trust, not distrust, is the first step at moving in that direction. **Trust begets trust.**

In our fast-paced, computer-driven world where we are always rushing to get things done faster and achieve success based on the bottom line, **trust is hard to come by**. We have learned that our government doesn't necessarily do what it says it is doing. Corporations will do almost anything to fake success and forget the bond of trust that the employees holding onto the rope might have. Loss of trust has made us cynical and negative. But what we are really losing is faith – faith that the people who run our government and corporations are who they say they are and doing what they say they are doing. **What we**

really want is honesty and authenticity ... then we can **trust.**

The Story of Josh

I was once involved with a rock climbing exercise at a Ronald McDonald House-sponsored cancer camp called *One Step at a Time*. The kids in our group were inner city teens with cancer. They had experienced lots of physical pain and suffering, and social rejection from their peers in the school system. I found myself looking at them and marveling at their strength, their resolve to fight, and their carefree gentle attitudes.

Our little group of ten started our rock climbing experience by attempting the climbing wall – a 60-foot wall dotted with imitation rock outcroppings that are used as stepping stones and hand holds. Like most kids, these teens were excited to try this adventure. They had a choice to climb the wall, or abstain with no judgment. Everyone tried it with varying degrees of success.

Josh, a twelve-year-old bone cancer amputee, was hanging in the background until the end. Reluctantly, he decided he would go ahead, explaining to us that he had a fear of heights. He decided that he would like to try the wall blindfolded so he wouldn't have to look down: A way to face his fear in **his own way**. Even though he had only one leg and was afraid of heights, he was willing to trust that his friends would show him the way.

First, Josh picked his belayer. (The belayer is the person who holds the rope attached to the climbing harness. If the climber falls, the belayer stops the fall by applying pressure to the rope.) Josh picked a special person as his belayer – a boy much younger than himself who had a seizure in front of the group just that morning at breakfast. It's an embarrassing experience for anybody, and one that destroys self-esteem. Somehow Josh knew his friend needed to be supported as much as he did.

As Josh started up the wall, he got to the first little rock outcropping. All at once, the kids shouted at him to let him know where to place his hands and foot, to boost himself up. He couldn't understand what any of them were saying because everyone was talking at once. So the kids devised a way to give him instruction by relaying messages to each other, with one boy responsible for relaying them to Josh.

At one point, Josh's body started to shake with fear. The kids shouted to encourage him to keep going, and before long the shaking stopped and Josh was on his way again. Near the top of the wall, Josh became stuck on a large outcropping. For a long time, he tried to figure out where to put his hands, and then suddenly, with a jolt, he propelled himself over it and to the top. His friends and support group were there to give him cheers and high fives when he descended.

After Josh was lowered to the ground, we discussed exactly how he felt about his accomplishment. He said, "I learned that this wall is like my cancer. When I get to the top, I've either lived or died – in any case it's the path that's the hard part. It's important that people communicate with me so that I can understand them. I can't understand when everyone is talking at the same time and I need to tell them that. I need to ask for help when I need it because it's so much easier when I have support of my friends. Finally I learned that the biggest obstacle of all was the one that made me strong enough to propel me to the top … and success. I can do anything I put my mind to doing."

Climbing a mountain and facing challenges require faith in oneself, determination, and especially the encouragement and help from friends. Josh certainly learned some wonderful life lessons from his friends – lessons he would never have learned had he not been in a tough time of his life.

"Grief knits two hearts with closer bonds than happiness ever can and common sufferings are far stronger links than common joys" — **Alphonse de LaMontine**

With a Little Help From My Friends

The belay system used on the mountain teaches us about relationships and friendships. It, combined with the rope system, is based on unconditional support and the heart connection. A unique communication system reminds the climbers of that relationship as they start the climb.

After the equipment has been prepared, harnesses are on and everything has been checked and rechecked for safety, the climber gets in position to start the climb:

The climber says to the belayer:

"ON BELAY?" which means, "Are you there?"
The belayer answers:
"BELAY ON!" which means, "I'm ready to help you."
The climber then says to the belayer:
"CLIMBING!" which means, "I'm going!"
The belayer answers:
"CLIMB ON!" which means, "Go ahead. You can trust me. I'm here."

Think about who your belayers are: God, friends, family. They are:

•Those who support you no matter what;

•Those you can communicate with openly and honestly;

•Those who encourage you;

•Those who give you permission to make mistakes and not judge you;

•Those who accept you unconditionally;

•Those who listen;

•Those who encourage you to be better;

•Those you can learn from.

Solid friendships and belayers can actually prolongs your life. A Kaiser Permanente report states that social support prolongs life, improves immune responses, and speeds recovery from trauma. One study showed that "socially isolated people are *three times* more likely to die than people who are connected and have good friendships, no matter what their ages."

I can't think of my friends without thinking of the quaking aspen trees. They have shallow roots that intertwine with other aspen trees. The older, stronger aspens nourish and support the younger, weaker ones. When fire comes, the roots shoot out suckers. The suckers add to the maze of roots under the ground. The tree dies, but the root maze is still connected for strength and support.

In transition, **surrounding yourself with YES people can save your life**. My friend Nancy is a YES person. She was my business partner and a master at coming up with spontaneous, hysterical one-liners under pressure, when the going got tough. She comes from a large Italian family, so she has been to more wakes and funerals than anyone I know. Her family loves a good wake.

Nancy and I had spent the whole day together doing business and our lives were ticking along just like usual. Tom was at home with a simple case of the flu ... or so I thought. When I came home that night to find Tom dead on the bed, it was no surprise that Nancy was the one I called. She handles tragedy *so* well, and I figured, she just *had* to be experienced at ambulances, coroners, and funeral homes.

Our behavior that night was bizarre. We handled it mechanically, moment by moment, with absolutely no emotion, as if this kind of thing happened to us every day. It was a form of shock, but the paramedics followed us both around in case the bomb finally dropped and we fell into a heap. You see, when Nancy is under stress, she cleans. So she took the broom and swept the driveway as the autumn leaves fell fast and furiously. I walked next to her, chattering mindlessly, with the paramedic hovering behind both of us. When the coroner arrived with his black baseball hat and leather jacket with CORONER printed in yellow, we started to panic. Reality hit us. And then the grief process started.

Two weeks later Nancy was with me when I started unloading the material possessions that I couldn't afford to hang on to. All the other losses that came on the heels of that first one, I shared with her. I threw her the rope and she rescued me ... with one-liners, a sense of humor, and the experience of a true Italian.

Intellectual support came from my friend Will and his wife Tricia. We all grew up together and had a strong bond. Will is the paramount businessman – serious to the bone, smart and organized. He organized my finances for me and taught me how to prepare the taxes. He went through my insurance to make sure I was okay. I threw Will the rope … and he took it and held me.

Heroes

I can't talk about throwing the rope without mentioning the importance of heroes, who are the rescuers in our lives. Sometimes we know them, and sometimes we don't, but they represent possibilities of what we may become.

⬥During my transition, my heroes were those who had gone before on the same path, searching for the meaning behind life's challenges. They helped me find ways to reinvent myself. They gave me hope and something to shoot for.

⬥Some heroes I'd read about. Many authors wrote about their own experiences and transformed their misfortune into an opportunity to help others. I never met them … and never will. They took the rope and pulled me up.

⬥My heroes were the cancer kids. They faced major disappointment, pain, and uncertain futures, with hope and positive attitudes.

⬥My heroes were those people I met who had lost jobs and were destitute, but kept trying every day, taking small jobs beneath them to make ends meet.

⬥My hero is my brother-in-law Bill who helped me financially and tried to do it anonymously so he would never get credit.

⬥My heroes are my friends who loved me, even when I did really dumb things. They demonstrated friendship and humanity by example and helped me find my footing at an unstable time.

Survival Tips

❖Find your team. Who is on your team? Make a list for the different aspects of your life: home, work, church, school, etc. Define your own role in relation to others on your team. What special things do you bring to the team?

❖Determine the common bond (the rope). What holds your team together? Are you going together in the same direction and at the same pace? Do you share common goals and values with your team ... your friends ... your support group?

❖Form your personal support group. Draw four concentric circles, one inside the other with the smallest in the center. In the middle circle write the names of those closest to you: your closest friends/relatives who you can say anything to. In the next circle, put your second closest friends/relatives, etc. You may be surprised to find that the inner circle has very few people in it ... and they may not be the ones you would expect.

❖Ask for help. Some people have a hard time asking for what they need. But how will people know how to help you if you don't ask? Most people, although they don't always know how, would love to help. It makes them feel good, too.

❖Join focus groups with those who have lost loved ones, jobs, a pet, or are facing serious illness ... whatever your challenge might be. This doesn't feel right for everyone, but try it. You may find the help you need.

❖Connect with others and turn your need into a way to help others. Try going out of your way to connect with old friendships that have slipped away. Try to contact those who are afraid to talk to you for whatever reason. Give them a chance to re-enter your friendship circle.

◈**Look for commonalities** with people you meet every day. You may find that you have something in common with the most unlikely people. Commonality brings instant connection. If you are introverted and have a hard time making early connections, gravitate towards an outgoing person and let THEM make the first step.

◈**Become a listener.** Ask questions and really care about the answers. Try a test run just once by asking questions of strangers you might meet casually during the day. Notice how people will open up to you if you care about them. This process will get easier and easier with practice.

◈**Find your belayers.** Think about who these people might be. Who would you throw the rope to? Talk to that person about the belay cues and how you could translate them to your situation. When you need someone to help you, this person will be ready.

◈**Get rid of your poisonous friends.** We all have those friends who sap us of energy and take too much. During transition, put these people in the outer circle. Take care of yourself, and surround yourself with YES people.

◈**Identify your YES people.** Go out of your way and establish a heart connection with some YES people. These are the unconditional friends who accept you as you are … and connect to your soul.

◈**Think of the individuals you love to associate with.** Notice the similarities between them. What does that tell you about how you want to be? Who you want to associate with? Who your encouragers are?

◈**Identify your heroes.** Put a picture of them somewhere so you can be reminded of someone who has inspired you. Sometimes this will spark you into the positive mode, and if you become negative, it will remind you that there is always a brass ring to reach for.

Part III
Thriving

"After climbing a great hill, one only finds that there are many more hills to climb. I have taken a moment here to rest, to steal a view of the glorious vista that surrounds me, to look bak on the distance I have come. But I can rest only for a moment, for with freedom comes responsibilities and I dare not linger... for my long walk is not yet ended." — **Nelson Mandela**

Chapter Eleven

Climbing to the Peak

"Life can only be understood backwards, but it must be lived forward." — **Kierkgaard**

As with all climbs—transitions, projects, business searches, or finding yourself again—the hardest part of the climb is the last five percent. It's "closing the sale" after you've been working hard to get a big corporation to buy your new computer software. It's the last ten yards between the ball placement and the goal line in a football game. You're almost there ... but it's cold, you're tired, it's steep, and you're struggling to survive. This is when all the excuses kick in ... the last five percent.

The final sprint is when the climb and the lessons learned from it come to light. This is when surviving turns into thriving. In spite of the adverse conditions, you have survived and have pulled through. Now you know you can do it. Thriving is growing beyond mere survival towards finding prosperity.

We learn that the mountain climb is an ongoing process. We are always climbing because the mountain always changes and evolves, just as we always change and evolve. We are as alive as the mountain. Getting to the peak is learning from the struggles and challenges, and finding the reward of new self-growth ... **AGAIN AND AGAIN.**

Gifts Along the Way

From the mountain we have learned that:

- Failure does not exist.
- We each have a spark of new life within us waiting to sprout.
- We can survive if we are prepared.
- We will travel faster and more efficiently if we lighten our load.
- Our attitude is a choice we make.
- Risks can result in great rewards.
- We need to take one step at a time.
- We will encounter obstacles along the way.
- We need each other for support.
- We can push to the peak.
- If we can survive this, we can survive anything.

We have seen that the world is full of possibilities and learned what works and what doesn't work. The world is larger now ... our comfort zone and boundaries have been expanded. Our preconceived notions about how the world should be, and those things from the past that have stopped us, are no longer valid. Instead, we see the world of new combinations and new possibilities through new eyes.

Most importantly, the noise has quieted down. After transition, the pace of life changes. Stillness and introspection replace the frantic search for security and self-discovery. In the stillness, we find security.

Synchronicity

When we give up control ... slow down ... wake up... and listen, the most amazing things happen. They are coincidences that seem meaningfully related but happen when we least expect it. When we are most vulnerable, quiet, and most awake to receive them, they appear.

The Gift of the Eagle Feather

Shortly after my husband's death, I ventured out on a solo thirty-day kayaking adventure in Prince William Sound, Alaska. Perhaps my deeper mission was to escape the emotional talons of grief, but, in fact, I was going back to my nature roots to find what peace and emotional balance I could in a life that had just been turned upside down and inside out.

While I was crossing the Sound in my well-packed kayak, a furious storm rolled in with a vengeance, relentlessly pounding me with driving rain, violent winds, and huge swells. Tossed around by the heaving water, I struggled to keep my tiny craft pointed into the wind. The howling gale made forward progress impossible. The rain pelted me, the drops stung my face and exposed hands like thousands of pinpricks. My arm muscles screamed as I fought to stay stable and upright until the fast-moving storm blew over.

Suddenly, a patch of blue sky appeared in the thinning clouds, and the sky began to brighten a little. *Aahhhhh!* ... Finally, a ray of hope that this torture would soon end. I looked up and saw a lone eagle, seemingly as disoriented as me, yet pushing forward to find an air current that would carry it safely to land. My eyes were glued on the bird, as if it was the only hope of "home" for me in this angry, empty, tumultuous place. Just then, it lost a tail feather and the wind died down. The eagle feather drifted down, skittishly. Then it found a strong air current, as if to beckon me. Finally, it changed pace, cradled gently down ... and, against all odds, came to rest on the bow of my unsteady kayak.

Privileged by such a gift, I smiled and relaxed my whole body. With strange new confidence and self-assurance, I paddled on effortlessly, finding a new untapped source of energy. Just a few minutes later, the sun shone through and the waters calmed.

When I departed Alaska three weeks later, I learned the significance of the eagle's gift. While waiting to board a train in Whittier, I entered a small shop. A book displayed on a pedestal was open, and this is what I read:

> *"In native American cultures the eagle was considered a sacred messenger who had the power to touch the Great Spirit. The feather of an eagle represents*

connection with the divine, and is a sacred healing tool. It symbolizes the state of grace which is achieved through hard work, and completion of the tests of initiation which result in taking personal power. Because you have experienced the highs and lows in life and learned to trust the connection to the Great Spirit, you are given the ability to understand the meaning of sacred journey.

"Eagle feather brings you light and teaches you to look higher; to reach with your heart to the Grandfather Sun and to love the shadow as well as the light. You will be given the ability to see beauty in both.

"The eagle feather promises that if you attack your own fear of the unknown, the wings of your soul will be supported by strong and gentle breezes which are the breath of the Great Spirit.

"Then you, like the eagle, will take flight."

Meaningful coincidences drop into our lives when we don't even notice them, and they pass us by. But in the vulnerable state of transition, we are most awake to the world around us. Pearls are dropped on our path and *now* we see them. Sometimes they come in the form of people who just appear and impact our lives forever. For example, a friend of mine needed $2,500 to pursue a dream she thought about for many years. Then she won it, just like that … in a drawing. Exactly $2,500!

Your intentions meet providence … and there you are!

The Gift of the Christmas Tree

I was married 29 years. Every year, without exception, we went through the same routine of buying a Christmas tree. I would get the house clean and ready to receive the tree. I'd get the Christmas music ready for action in the CD player next to the fireplace. I'd go to the grocery store and buy bags full of hors d'oeuvres and bottles of spiced apple cider to fix as soon as we got back with the tree. When the children were small we had a wonderful time with all this fanfare.

As the years passed and the children became teenagers, the Christmas tree tradition ceased to be fun. The three boys would rather stay home and watch a football game or be with their friends than tramp through a tree lot in the cold looking for a tree, and *then* spend hours with their parents listening to Christmas music, drinking cider, and eating hors d'oeuvres.

The year after Tom died, only my youngest boy came home from college for a lonely Christmas with just me. I was determined to make it a traditional Christmas for him in at least a few small ways. The day before he was to return home, I made my regular trek to the grocery store for the hors d'oeuvres and cider. I put them neatly in the kitchen and then carefully placed the Christmas music CDs next to the fireplace and CD player.

Off I went with my checkbook, Christmas music for the car, and my ball of twine to tie the tree onto the car. I drove to the local tree lot. I parked the car, and … I couldn't move. I was frozen and the tears started falling. I just couldn't do it. It wasn't the same. My husband was gone and so was the tradition and all of those warm comfortable Christmas tree feelings.

I decided to breathe deeply and set off for another tree lot. I drove two towns over to a place I had never been so there would be no memories. I blasted out Christmas music in the car as high as it would go and finally pulled into a parking spot right in front. This time I got the car door part of the way open, put one foot on the ground, and … the tears started to fall again. I still couldn't do it. I told myself: "Okay, Cheryl, you have to go into this lot and get the tree." But I couldn't, so I decided to take care of myself and put it off for another day.

I decided to drive to the town I had moved from about four months earlier. My friend had stored my Christmas decorations at her house there and at least I could pick them up and get *something* done. I also knew those boxes were waiting for me outside of her house so I wouldn't have to face anyone with puffy red eyes. The one-hour drive to Barrington was silent. As promised, the boxes were sitting outside her house waiting for me. Mission accomplished! "Okay, I'll get the tree tomorrow."

As I silently started to drive home, I noticed the old Christmas tree farm lot where Tom and I had bought our trees for many years. I took a deep breath and drove in the driveway. I was the only car there. Just as I drove up a farmer smiling broadly came out of the little farmhouse.

"Oh, hi," he said. "We were hoping you would come. I have a tree here in the corner waiting for you. We heard you moved away and were hoping you would come to get a tree. Your husband really lit up our lives every year with his big smile. We were so sad to hear that he had passed away, and we just want to give you this perfect tree to show you that we care."

I just stood, dropped-jaw, feeling incredible gratitude. He'd cut the bottom off the tree straight and flat because he knew I probably didn't have a saw at home, wrapped it in a plastic sheath, and instructed me on how to get it up the elevator and in the stand ... and I didn't even know his name.

When you have reached for and tried, and that "something" is still beyond your reach, when you know it's right but you just can't get it together ... *boom* ... Providence steps in to give you an extra push. You had better listen ... and answer ... because you have been given the gift of clarity.

Not Getting It All

We don't get it all. I can think of plenty of things I thought I wanted but never happened. And it's a darned good thing. **These are the gifts of the unanswered prayer.** I wanted to meet a replacement soul mate soon after Tom died. The best gift I received was that prayer *not* being answered until the time was right. Having a relationship before being ready and attaching to someone while still vulnerable often leads to a rebound mismatch. Taking the wrong job before you're ready can lead to disaster, too. **The right answers come when the time is right and you are ready to receive.**

Tom 2

I had met my share of dysfunctional men. There was Prince Charming the cheater, the senator, the professor, the plumber, the professional water skier, and the alcoholic. The crowning blow was the blind date with the confessed *child molester*. Then I was done.... No more dating for me. Finito! Finally I admitted that I was happy with what I had. My speaking business was fine, I loved where I lived, and had a lot of great friends. I was self-sufficient, enjoying the single life, and doing well ... *and then ... BOOM ... it happened!*

A simple tennis event set me on the same side of the net with a widower – a sweet guy by the name of Tom who lost his wife about the same time I lost my husband. Later into the evening at a casual pizza dinner, by "coincidence," we found ourselves sitting together. We bonded over our commonalities and similar interests. Four days later, I left for a trip to Austria with a ski club. Providence stepped in. Sitting next to me on the plane ... and in the same ski club group ... was Tom 2. *It was a done deal!*

I had heard from day one that grief and healing are full of surprises. Meeting Tom 2 was not my choice. It wasn't his either. It was handed to us. We both were awake and ready to receive.

Closure

I wanted closure. I wanted to get over the agony of transition, close the door on it, and move on with my life. But I learned that closure is not about closing the door on the past life and moving on. It's not about forgetting. It's not about accepting what you've been through and saying goodbye. **There is no closure to the grief process.** No matter how long it goes on, it's still a part of you. It pops up and you feel the pain again, but in a different way. **Closure in transition is accepting that the pain is part of who you are.** Now I look back, see the good things, and honor them. I carry the grief process with me and know it is always part of me. It has made me who I am today.

Closure is coming to terms with reality. Accepting the truth of the situation is hard. I know the families of the victims of 9-11 suffer from the lack of *proof* that their loved ones were victims. The physical proof provides closure that nothing else can. The proof brings our loss into consciousness and helps us find meaning in it. It allows us to make sense out of the experience and put it in perspective. The questions about *how* the person died is a closure that many 9-11 families will never get.

Not saying goodbye is an important part of healing. The 9-11 families never got to say goodbye. Those people who have lost jobs often don't either. Leaving without saying goodbye makes us feel insignificant and unimportant. It trivializes the relationship and the past, as if it just vanishes without the proper ending.

The Gift of the Cardiologist

The closure I was searching for ... I found. Closure came for me on an airplane bound for Arkansas about two years after Tom died. Next to me was a kind man reading the by-laws for the American Heart Association. We chatted briefly as perfect strangers do. As time went on, our conversation moved from heart health to working with cancer kids, and then to family. He asked me about my family. I described my children and my deceased husband. He asked me some questions about how my husband died. My answer: myocarditis, or inflammation of the heart. And then he gave me the most wonderful gift possible.

He said: "You couldn't have revived him if you tried. There was nothing anyone could do. A hemorrhaging heart needs to be replaced. It can't be fixed. He would have needed a heart transplant. He would have been on a heart-and-lung machine, and then put on a long list. Then you wait ... and wait ...and wait. Many on the list die. Active people like him have a hard time getting through this. Given his condition, you're probably lucky that you saved him a lot of agony and frustration."

His honest words allowed me to put some perspective on Tom's death ... that fate had dealt us a blow we had no choice about. His life was over! I finally felt like I could move on. Closure came for me, then and there, in the guise of a well-known heart surgeon.

Putting It All Together

Going through transition is like the scary feeling of standing on a ledge, teetering, and trying to get our footing. We feel as if we may fall any minute. It's like standing on one leg and having the other one pulled out from under us. Our whole body shifts to help us stabilize. **Our mind and body work together to help us balance.** In transition, we are trying to get our legs back, to be stable and balanced with all our parts connected. The last 5% of the climb is when we are finally able to do that.

Our lives are made up of many different parts. They are all connected and sometimes … disconnected. The climb of transition has dictated that some parts of our lives have been neglected as we struggle to find our footing. Now, as we climb to the peak, we get our perspective and balance back.

Regaining balance is about refocusing on all the parts of our life and putting them together:

- Financial
- Physical
- Career
- Family and friends
- Personal growth
- Spiritual
- Recreational
- Health

If you've lost a job, climbing the mountain to a new career path is your focus. Your family life may have suffered. Maybe you haven't made the time to think about your spiritual life. With job recovery, the career and financial parts of your life improve. You are planting your feet. **Climbing to the peak is about finally standing on both feet, looking at all the parts of our lives, and finding the whole person.**

Connecting to the Universe

The clearest way to find ourselves is to connect to the world beyond ourselves. Spirituality is not about religious practice or doctrine. **Spiritual growth is about finding our part in the larger whole, seeing the big picture, and acknowledging that there is a presence of life that holds us all**

together. Finding our spirituality is finding meaning and purpose in our lives as part of that whole, where we fit in, and why we are here.

Seeing Cycles

The universe is made up of constant cycles: life–death–life … joy–suffering–joy … darkness–light–darkness. The cycles always repeat themselves … and always will. They are the natural order of things and are thus predictable. They are part of our lives, everyone around us, and the natural world. Realizing that change is constant and a natural process frees us to experience all changes with the hope of another change coming.

A natural order and rhythm also exists. We see many examples of order in nature. Take water, for example. No new water is ever formed. Instead, it cycles itself constantly. It is under ground and bubbles up in springs to form rivers. It ends up in a reservoir and then our faucets. It's discharged back into the river, whence it flows to the sea, and evaporates into the atmosphere. This forms clouds that make rain come down onto the earth and feed the river again. Or the rain may cool and become snow that feeds a glacier, where it stays for millennia. Then one day, the glacier falls into the ocean as an iceberg. Or the rain is used by plants and trees to grow leaves that transpire the water back into the atmosphere, where it may condense as fog. Water is a complex connected and interdependent system that never ends. We become a part of this system as we drink and use the water.

Seeing Your Place

Seeing your place is seeing where you fit in amidst the whole; it shows you what is available in this world of possibilities outside of yourself. Although your relative insignificance is obvious, you are able to make a contribution in some small way. By practicing respect for the environment and actively working to conserve our resources, you can make a small contribution to the environment you are a part of. You can take what nature gives you … and give back again.

Transition brings an internal shift in the way we see the world and the way we relate to the world and each other. The shift comes on slowly and quietly. Once the noise subsides and leaves peace in its wake, we are able to see the peak. We are now awake enough to see the beauty of the sunrise because we have experienced the darkness of night. We are creative enough to see the rainbow, even during the rain. We have moved and changed:

> From Fear ➜ To Faith
> From Hostility ➜ To Hospitality
> From Sadness ➜ To Joy
> From Pessimism ➜ To Optimism
> From Self ➜ To Others

Survival Tips

◈**Don't give up.** Make sure to look back and see how far you've come. Do whatever you have to do to make it to the peak. It will be hard, but you've made it this far, so use the help of others to make the final five percent.

◈**Balance.** Identify which parts of your life you neglected during your transition process. Sometimes it helps to take the eight major aspects of your life and rate them on a scale of 1 to 10:

- Financial
- Physical
- Career
- Family and friends
- Personal growth
- Spiritual
- Recreation
- Health

Then rate where you are with them. How satisfied are you with where you are right now? Follow your awareness with a little action and try to balance yourself a little more.

◈**Synchronicity.** It happens and you don't even notice it sometimes. Think about the meaningful coincidences you have experienced. Make a list and you will see how lucky you are. The list will also help you notice when they happen.

◈**Appreciate nature.** Take long walks alone by the river, up the mountain, or in a quiet neighborhood. Walk slowly and take it all in. If you stop once in a while and look around, you may see the world of nature open up for you.

Chapter Twelve

Soaring!

*"What we have done for ourselves dies with us.
What we have done for others lives on"....*
— **William Pine**

When the eagle soars, he opens his wings and lets the winds carry him where he will go. Soaring over and above the mountain, he uses the uplift of the unseen wind to hold him up ... a force he has learned to trust. He sees the world with new eyes and with new wisdom. From above he is able to see that everything is connected and that there is unity in the world below him. He is set free with the knowledge of his place in the universe. It all makes sense now.

He has reached his mountain peak, and is going on ... over and above. He will encounter other challenges in his path of survival. He will struggle, feel anguish and physical pain, and then he will flap his mighty wings and soar ... again. Life is a struggle ... life is difficult. We are all here to experience it, to go through transition and change, to learn the lessons along the way, and to find new vision and new perspective. **The purpose of hard times is to transform the challenges into something greater than we started with.** It is only then that we are able to be truly happy ourselves.

"True happiness is when our greatest talent meets the world's greatest needs."— Frederick Bruechner, American theologian

Transition is a spiritual movement that teaches us that we are all searching for the same things: to love and be loved, to feel comfortable and at home where we are, to be appreciated and valued. **We are searching to make a difference in this life so that the world is a better place because we lived.** Taking our new wisdom to others and helping them with their struggles gives our lives meaning and strength. Extending compassion to them gives them love and gives us love in return.

Our greatest joy is found in extending our talents to those in darkness—to those we have ignored and pretended not to notice, those we were afraid to look in the eye for fear they would ask something of us. Happiness is found in giving to those we meet along the way … especially those who have no way. We who have been lost can show others hope and a way to be found by living compassionately.

The Sherpas of Nepal

The Sherpas of Nepal are small people with dark skin and bright pink cheeks … a poor yet happy people. They are easy-going and always smiling amid the trials of their everyday life, carrying heavy loads up and down mountains with massive yaks at their side. They wear no shoes as they climb over rocks and ice.

I cannot think of the virtue of compassion without thinking of them. They are charitable, mild-mannered, and tolerant. They do not value financial wealth, material possessions, position, power, or fame. They are not a focused, forceful, and driven people. Instead, the Sherpa definition of success is to pass into the next life having made the lives of as many people around them as rich as possible. When a Sherpa greets you, he makes compassionate eye contact, smiles with his hands together in prayer position, and says, "Namasté," which means:
"I salute that place in you where the entire universe resides: all peace, all love, all joy. When I am in that place in me, and you are in that place in you … WE ARE ONE."

In our culture, living the Sherpa example of compassion is difficult. In fact, if we were to take what we have learned from transition and do just that, we would have functional teams at work, have companies that excel at customer service, and family members who care more about each other than themselves. We would have a society made up of individuals with the emphasis on *service,* not *self*-service.

The Hero's Journey

Many in our culture see life as a linear experience. It's a one-dimensional approach: We have a goal and we achieve it, cause leads to effect, new leads to old. We live and then we die. We search for something and we find it. In transition, we feel pain and go through adjustment and a new life begins.

Joseph Campbell, in *The Hero's Journey,* sees life another way. The journey of life is a cycle that doesn't end. It perpetuates itself in another way. We have a goal ... we achieve it ....and then we share it. In transition, we feel pain and go through adjustment to a new life ... and then we share what we have learned. In nature, the cycle of life goes from life to death ... and then back to life again. It's a circular path.

Those of us who have been through tough times have been on a personal hero's journey of transition that is like the climb up the mountain. The climb does not end when we reach the peak. Instead, we go beyond and soar by sharing our lessons with others ... **and then we climb again.** Every time, we experience more, learn more, and eventually soar again. Because we have climbed our mountain, we are able to live with passion and compassion ... and have something meaningful to share.

In mythology, the hero's journey is made up of three stages:
1. **The call to adventure ... the beginning of birth to new life**.

> In our lives, this is the time when we are called to climb the mountain. Our challenge is put before us. We face grief, loss, and break away from the past.

2.The threshold ... the battles and obstacles.

In our lives, we meet physical and emotional obstacles along the way. These are the tests that teach us what we have yet to learn. We face them and overcome them with spiritual help. This is when synchronicity happens and we see our place in the whole. This is the point of transformation.

3.The return with the prize ... getting the prize and sharing it.

In our lives, we find ourselves new and changed and are now able to use that rebirth for the good of others by sharing what we have learned. This is the purpose of the whole journey. The challenge turns into something greater and gives the journey meaning.

SOARING!

Sharing the Lessons
(VICTORY)

Our purpose is clear. To SHARE WHAT WE
HAVE LEARNED for the good of others.

I. The Call to Adventure
(BIRTH)

CHANGE HAPPENS and the
CHALLENGE is put before
us. Life as we knew it has
ended.

III. Rebirth

NEW LIFE BEGINS....
We have learned from the struggles
of life. We start to live again, with
new wisdom .

II. THE THRESHOLD
(LIFE)

We endure PHYSICAL AND
EMOTIONAL OBSTA-
CLES. We climb and strug-
gle as we try to find new life.

SPIRITUAL HELP
(SYNCHRONICITY)

With spiritual help we are able to
OVERCOME OUR OBSTACLES and
SEE OUR PLACE IN THE WHOLE.

"The wise man does not lay up his own treasures. The more he gives to others, the more he has found his own."— **Lao Tzu**

The Mountain You Have Climbed

After preparing, working, and struggling to climb a mountain, we know one thing for sure: We will always encounter more mountains to climb. No matter what our stage in life, the biggest mountain in our way is always yet to be climbed. That mountain is ourselves.

❖ As we constantly try to improve ourselves, we will constantly be climbing.

❖ As things happen to us in our lives and we need to change our way of thinking and being, we will be climbing.

❖ As relationships change, we will be climbing.

❖ As we succeed and fail to reach our goals, we will change them, and we will be climbing.

❖ As we experience more and more … we will be climbing.

We have learned to see the challenges in our lives as opportunities for adventure and positive change. We have learned how to climb a mountain and:

- How to wander in the foothills and find ourselves;
- How to see our vision;
- How to prepare for survival;
- How to choose the adventure attitude;
- How to take risk and see out of the comfort zone;
- How to travel one step at a time;
- How to overcome obstacles;
- How to throw the rope to others when we need it;
- How to reach the peak;
- How to SOAR!

NAMASTE!

Survival Tips

◆ **Think of your hero's journey.** What have you learned? How have you changed? How will your experiences make your next journey different?

◆ **Serve others.** Find ways you can serve others that are compatible with the skills you have learned along the way ... or skills that may have been hidden that you can dig up ... or skills you have honed all of your life.

I AM AN EAGLE

By Mickey Olsen and Mickey Fadler

Three miles high
On a snow covered peak
He unfurls his wings
And he is free

Alone at dawn
While the rest of the world
Is still fast asleep
He is soaring

Where the wind and the sky collide
There is the place you will find him
Born with a passion – a dream in his heart

He cries, "I AM AN EAGLE … AND I FLY.."

Deep inside
I know that god
Placed me on this earth
For a reason

Awake my soul
The time is at hand
I will find the courage
To rise above

Where the joy inside me comes to life
That's where believers can find me
Born with a passion – a dream in my heart

Say " I AM AN EAGLE .. AND I FLY"

The Survival Tips Index

You're alive. Do something. The directive in life, the moral imperative was so uncomplicated. It could be expressed in single words, not complete sentences. It sounded like this: Look. Listen. Choose. Act.

Anonymous

It's okay to be mad, but think long and hard about acting on your anger! Burning bridges behind you and causing others pain is non-productive and could come back to bite you some day. Let the feelings pass and move out of it.

Let yourself feel fully and completely. It's okay to go through a roller coaster of emotions. In fact, it's totally normal if you do. Feel the emotions and let them roll over you. At first they are overwhelming, but as time passes, it gets easier and you feel better afterwards.

Be sad. Allow yourself to be sad and beware of the urge to "stuff" your feelings. Eventually stuffed feelings must come out. Better they come out during the grief process and not at an inappropriate time in the future.

Denial is okay. It protects you and gives you time to recuperate before you deal with your new situation. The funny thing about denial is that you don't even know you are in it, and you may let it go too long without knowing it.

Honor the past. Get out the pictures and honor what was. Don't dwell on it, but honor and remember the good things. They are an important part of who you are.

Seek wise guidance. If you need help, try support groups. Grief groups are great and are all different. Search for one that's right for you. You'll find comfort knowing others are going through the same thing. Don't be discouraged if the first support group you try isn't right for you. I went to three support groups before I found a good one. Friends and family are great, too, but it's better to find others who are at a different stage of the process than you are.

Seek other survivors or someone you admire who has gone through the same kind of loss. This person is your "grief mentor" and confident. Common sufferings are far stronger links than common joys and you will find a sense of safety and communion with a person who has gone through the same type of experience.

Surround yourself with people who are "listeners," not talkers. That could be anyone. Even strangers can be good listeners.

HUGS...HUGS... HUGS! They say you need 8 hugs a day to be emotionally healthy. Ask your 'huggee' to HOLD ON TIGHT.

Pamper yourself. Take time off for yourself. A "shrink" friend told me to get massages after my husband died... and my friend, who was lonely after her child went off to college, was told the same thing. It will help you to stay 'in touch' with the outside world.   Spend money to pamper yourself. You're no good to anyone else if you aren't good to yourself. Here are a few suggestions:

Read grief books. They help you see that your experiences are normal. I know it's hard to concentrate on reading when you hurt. If it's hard for you, read in small chunks and give yourself permission to skip around.

Take care of yourself more than ever. This is a time to get a physical, take extra vitamins, and listen to your body when it tells you something is wrong. Eat lots of fruits and vegetables, and avoid obsessive eating that may make you feel even worse physically. Drink plenty of water.

Remember to breathe deep and strong. It's amazing what good, new air can do to replenish you. Breathing helps you center and stabilize yourself when your inside meets the outside. It also helps you let go of control and relax. Breathe in through your nose and out through your mouth. The air entering your nose actually spins down into the deep part of your lungs and results in a better use of the oxygen. You are also more likely to force all the "bad air" out and let it all go. When you feel as if you are losing it, just take a deep breathe and try to relax.

Exercise helps you let go and get through the day. Your physical and mental self feel better for the stress you release (see more about stress in Chapter 5). Establish some sort of exercise routine. When you treat exercise like a regular part of the day, just like brushing your teeth, you'll find it's easy to do.

Try meditation to silence the voices and get you in touch with a larger world. Create a special, sacred, comfy place just for you and go there to enjoy the silence. This also opens up your senses and gets you in touch with yourself.

Surround yourself with living things, such as plants, goldfish, fruit, and animals. Don't isolate yourself too much. It's good to be around people, even if you aren't socializing with them. Their presence is enough to keep you alive, too.

Surround yourself with lots of colors. Go for the bright, vivid colors to spark you up a bit: yellow, orange, red, and green. Avoid black and dark blue.

Go for professional help. There is nothing wrong with professional help. Counselors are great at looking at your situation objectively and giving you support. I went to a counselor when I felt especially desperate. Just like finding the right grief group, finding the right counselor is important.

Just be. Live in the moment and grab the good ones when they come. You will learn to appreciate them more than you ever did. You will also find that when you concentrate on those positive moments, they will eventually overshadow the negative ones.

Slow down. If you feel panic setting in, try to calm yourself down, sit back, and relax or distract yourself by doing something you enjoy. The feeling of being lost, alone, and out of control will pass with time.

Schedule yourself. I know it doesn't sound as if it goes with **just be**, but it does. If you have a schedule, you can space out the ugly parts of your life. Some people in transition mentally fly around all over the place and need to schedule a little so they can go on living, especially now, when they are more scattered than usual. A schedule will help you get out of bed, get things done, and help reduce the chaos.

No need to be a perfectionist. If you're sick of housework, chores, or tedious stuff, then don't do those things for a while. It's okay if your surroundings aren't perfect. I would love to tell you to forget the painful things such as the bills, but you simply must do some things. If you can't face the tough tasks, ask someone to help you. People love to help.

Affirmations are a great way to boost your self-worth. Say good things about yourself in the present tense, such as, "I'm really efficient. I can do anything I put my mind to," or "I'm fine on my own. The world is full of possibilities for me." Write them down and stick them on your mirror. Say them to yourself over and over. What you say becomes reality.

Find your comfort things. My friends bought me a full-length body pillow I affectionately named Robert Redford. He wore a hat and tie and stretched the whole length of the bed. My foot rested against him when I was asleep. He helped me feel less alone.

My friend, who went through a serious bout with cancer, received a bear from one of her friends. The bear sat with her through all of her treatments and recuperation. When she was cancer free, she passed the bear on to another friend, Barbara, when her husband died. She has it now and will pass it on when she is better.

Journal. Journaling does wonders in helping you clean out your head and work through your feelings and concerns. To get the most from journaling, follow these guidelines:

Allow yourself to do dumb things. You *will* do things that are out of character. Somebody told me I would, and I didn't believe them. I did them anyway. If you find yourself behaving this way, just make sure not to hurt yourself or other people in the process.

Watch the rebound. If you've lost a loved one, watch the rebound. We are all searching for love. I was lonely but grateful that I didn't meet someone when I was vulnerable and needy. You can get yourself in trouble by falling for the wrong person out of loneliness. Substituting one strong emotion for another may just postpone the grief you need to experience and learn from. If you have lost a job, be careful not to "jump" at the first one that comes along, especially if it isn't right for you.

Get up and move in the morning. Avoid the pitfall of sleeping too much, as it will cause you to become lethargic. Lethargy feeds on itself and before you know it, you'll spiral into total inactivity. To be healthy and fit, the body needs rest, but it also needs to move and function.

Have a structure. In your job or in your old life, you had a routine/structure that you were accustomed to. Set up an interim structure to replace the old patterns and allow room for adjustment with some free time. This helps you get up in the morning, get moving, *and* makes you think more creatively.

Allow time to marinate. Just like a fine tea, you need time to steep. If you have lost a job, give yourself three to four weeks to steep: reassess, analyze, and take care of yourself. Get your personal head together before you get into the job search mode. Caution: This only works for a short time and can easily turn into procrastination.

Make a list of 50 things you enjoy doing. Write them down quickly, without thinking, to flush out your real desires. If you think too much, you tend to judge the items as you write them, and that stops you from finding your real passion. I found the first 25 were easy to write and the last 25 were harder. When done, though, you see a pattern and repetition to your list. Your passion will soon be apparent.

Determine what you're good at. Think of skills you were born with and those you have developed over the years. Think of hard skills and personality strengths you have developed. Are they compatible with what you want to do?

Determine what you need to do. What would you do if you only had six months to live?

Determine your personality traits. Is what you want compatible with the kind of person you are? Are you energized by being alone or with others? Do you like to be in control, or are you happy following? Are you always on the go, or do you like a slower pace?

Define your core values. Think about what really matters to you. What do you value? Are you living congruently with those values? Define them, and then prioritize them and make sure your vision is on target.

Tweak your passion. Think of all the creative ways you can tweak your passion and turn it into a life's work or a new lifestyle. You're just dreaming now, but this kind of creative thinking opens new doors of possibility for you.

Define your goals. What do you need to do to live your passion? Think of the steps you can take that will drive you in the right direction. Write down monthly goals, weekly goals, and daily goals. Go from there to immediate goals.

Connect your goals to rewards. Think of each goal individually and connect it to the rewards or satisfaction you will get by achieving that goal. Will it be fun to complete? Will you feel more secure if you do it? Will you feel power, excitement, or pleasure? Write down each one. Once you think in terms of rewards, your goals will be much easier to strive for.

Learn all you can. Study, study, study. Take classes to open up possibilities, but don't overburden yourself. Pressure on top of pressure can turn into blow-up. When you grieve, you will notice that it is hard to concentrate. So, if you can, take something enjoyable and easy to get into the study/learning mode little by little. You'll find it can be fun.

Make a serious exercise schedule. Start out slow. Make sure your schedule is doable and not too hard or too long. You will find working out easier every day, and it will become a routine before you know it. Exercise does wonders for your physical and emotional well-being.

Simplify. Think of the things you carry with you. What can you unload? Make a list of all the things you don't need. At my workshops, I have people write these things on separate pieces of paper and then trash them. You'll be surprised how freeing it is to symbolically throw this stuff away once and for all.

Try to stop worrying about things you can't change. If you are a worrier and find it hard to stop, ask for help from others. You can even ask for professional help. Sometimes a person with an objective point of view will help you to gain a healthy perspective.

Set your sights forward, not backward. Remember to look ahead, not behind you. Look at the road ahead and envision the top of your mountain. Then, set your small steps (goals) along the way to help you get there.

Assess your relationships and determine who your "yes" people are. If you feel comfortable, let the "no" people know you can't handle them right now. I never had the courage to do that, so I just let those relationships fade out. Funny how more "yes" people showed up during my grief process. Today I have a group of wonderful new friends.

Make lists. Writing lists of daily duties and obligations will help you keep on track and avoid cluttering your day with too much, which could cause you to lose focus.

Rid your schedule of unnecessary obligations. What have you said "yes" to that makes your life cluttered and unmanageable? Attend to the necessary responsibilities and delegate the rest to others.

Clean your closets and your office. Uncluttering your physical surroundings will unclutter your head and leave you open to possibilities.

Reduce stress. Do whatever you need to in order to reduce stress. Stay away from negative things and people; seek positive friends, keep busy, exercise, and do fun recreational activities.

Try new things. Think of some fun, low-cost things you can do that you enjoy. Honor yourself by making time to do something just for you ... alone. Try to think like a child with a full world of possibility from which to choose.

Be fully present and notice how you approach life – positively or negatively. Once you notice when you are negative, change that mindset once a day. Increase the frequency of that change little by little, day-by-day. You will be amazed at how much better you feel, and how people react to you.

Create a gratitude journal. Positive thinking becomes natural for you when you think about what you are grateful for. Every evening, make a list of all the things you are grateful for. You will find that the more you write, the more youwill think in the positive. Example: "I am grateful for a beautiful cool morning, the flowers in my garden, the promise of rain, the smile on the face of the little boy I saw this morning, and the nice man I talked to in the coffee shop." Keep it simple. It will change your thinking.

Affirmations. I've mentioned this technique before, but it's critical that you say positive, uplifting, present tense statements frequently. Write a note to yourself with your affirmations on it and tape it on your mirror. When you look ridiculous, smiling at yourself in the mirror, you can remind yourself how awesome you are.

Try an attitude readjustment. Notice the good in things and ask yourself, "What am I supposed to learn from this?" Make a list of some of the bad things that have happened to you. Then, write how that changed your life for the good and what you learned from it. This will help you change your mindset.

Fake it till you make it. This may sound odd, but when you get up in the morning, look in the mirror. Put the biggest smile on your face, and hold it for at least ten seconds. Do it again several times during the day, especially when you find a negative thought creeping in. Surprisingly, you will find that happiness follows you when you start with a smile and positive thoughts.

Do the Dalai Lama Attitude check. In the morning, think of positive attitude intentions for the whole day. Check in the evening to see how you did. Did you approach your moments of the day with a positive frame of mind? Keeping your intentions close to mind peaks your awareness of how you approach life.

Reframe your attitude. Think of how you can reframe your challenges into something positive:

List your successes. Think of all the things you do right and what it was like to do them for the first time. Your comfort zone expands with the successes you have. Think of how big your comfort zone really is now. Define it and put your foot out of it, one toe at a time. It will get bigger and bigger.

Change some little things. We certainly are creatures of habit. To change your mindset and see things creatively, change some of the small habits and routines. Sit in a different place at the table when you eat, drink coffee without reading the newspaper, take the dog for a walk around the block in the opposite direction, or go to a completely different place. It's amazing but you will find yourself opening yourself up to creative thinking. In my workshops on creative thinking, I find people come up with amazing creative solutions to problems if they just change some of these small habits.

Do something scary. Think about what really frightens you, something that gives you a creepy feeling inside. Do that scary thing anyway. Take just the first small step. Have a back-up plan … tell people what you are doing, have them there for you … and then go for it.

Embark on a personal adventure. Take yourself on adventures, big or small. Do it alone and regularly. Make sure it's something a little different from anything you have done before. Put it on the calendar so you don't find a way to get out of it. You'll likely think of every excuse in the book not to, but DO IT. Tell people you are doing it so you follow through. When you finish with one adventure, schedule the next one so you have something to look forward to.

Take care of yourself now. It will make your heart beat a little faster and rejuvenate you.

Have a back-up plan. If you are afraid to make first step into new things, tell others, make sure you are prepared, and have a back-up plan so you feel safe. You'll find those attempts to move out of your comfort zone get easier and more successful every time.

Honor who you are. Make sure you listen to that inner voice that tells you how far you should go. It usually knows best.

Analyze your fears. Being in touch with what you are REALLY afraid of will help you put that fear into proper perspective

Realize that failure does not exist. We've all failed many times in our lives. Recheck those failures now. Were they lessons and gifts in disguise? What new beginnings came out of them? What lessons?

Try to do things alone. Try it little by little. There is no need to rush into it too quickly. Try something small at first, such as going to the movies. Once you get through the ticket line, you will be sitting in the dark, and are safe there. I found it to be a great way to get used to it.

Have faith. An unseen force always holds us up when we start to fall. Let go of control on things you can't control anyway, and have faith that you will be supported.

Allow yourself to just be. Being is all about relaxing. To appreciate each step on your path takes presence. Take a deep breath and relax … pay attention to what is going on around you … people, things and nature as it is right now. Notice how your body parts feel … where your legs and arms are … how your neck muscles feel. Let it all go and open up your senses.

Appreciate the moments. Think of all those amazing snippets of life that are happening to you, both good and bad. Think in terms of taking it one step at a time. Notice how far you have come.

Listen. Chart the sounds you hear around you either on paper or mentally. It will help you become more aware of your new surroundings. Listen for the small things.

Practice mindfulness. Dedicate time to think about the moments of the day. Analyze where your mind and body is in those moments.

Pace yourself. Slow yourself down. Remember, slow and steady wins the race. How do you slow yourself down? Take breaks, breathe, read a book, take a walk ... whatever makes you take a mind break. During the grief process, I found exercise to be a real vehicle in changing pace. After strenuous exercise, nothing feels better than the shower afterwards. A short walk will do the same thing. The exhale you feel after a change of pace gives you balance and helps you feel better.

Chunk. Make a list of all the things that challenge you now – ALL of them. Then prioritize them, chunk them into categories, and put them into little invisible boxes that you put on the shelf. Then, starting with box number one, take it down and handle it. Don't even think of the other boxes. You can take them down later. Soon, you'll notice the progress as your shelf empties.

Do small projects. Take on some small, relaxing projects that have nothing to do with your transition: creative projects such as woodworking or sewing, listen to or play music, art projects, gardening. Put yourself into them totally. Appreciate the moments while you do them.

Connect with nature. Nature shows us that we are part of a larger whole. Taking a walk, standing by the lake, or looking at a tree helps you feel a peaceful silence. You will feel more alive.

Silence the inner critic. Whenever you resort to negative self-talk, think about that inner critic sitting on your shoulder. Give him a face and slap him around. You might even draw him on a piece of paper and throw it right in the garbage. It sounds ridiculous, I know, but you will get a thrill out of getting rid of him, once and for all.

Keep an anger journal. If you are prone to anger, list all the things that make you angry on a daily basis … people, road rage, situations you might encounter every day. Be careful not to make your obstacles yourself. Can you think of another way to deal with it? Analyze what sets you off, and avoid those situations any way you can.

Concentrate on your positive emotional moments. Journal about them and remind yourself what they felt like and how they affected your behavior. Positive begets positive. Try to reframe your obstacles into opportunities for adventure and positive change.

Make a timeline. Make a list of the obstacles you've had to handle that you remember. If you are dealing with job loss, list all the tough situations at work you can recall. When you were most successful, how did you do it? How could you build on that next time around? If you are dealing with loss, what did you learn from past losses that can help you now? You'll be amazed at all the things you have survived. You'll discover that you are already an expert at survival.

List the past roadblocks you have handled. Could you have handled them differently in terms of positive attitude, patience, perspective, flexibility, and vision?

How controllable are the obstacles in your life? Can you change them by your own actions?

Identify daily obstacles. What are the daily obstacles in your way? Think of them objectively. What can you do to handle them now?

Find your team. Who is on your team? Make a list for the different aspects of your life: home, work, church, school, etc. Define your own role in relation to others on your team. What special things do you bring to the team?

Determine the common bond (the rope). What holds your team together? Are you going together in the same direction and at the same pace? Do you share common goals and values with your team ... your friends ... your support group?

Form your personal support group. Draw four concentric circles, one inside the other with the smallest in the center. In the middle circle write the names of those closest to you: your closest friends/relatives who you can say anything to. In the next circle, put your second closest friends/relatives, etc. You may be surprised to find that the inner circle has very few people in it ... and they may not be the ones you would expect.

Ask for help. Some people have a hard time asking for what they need. But how will people know how to help you if you don't ask? Most people, although they don't always know how, would love to help. It makes them feel good, too.

Join focus groups with those who have lost loved ones, jobs, a pet, or are facing serious illness ... whatever your challenge might be. This doesn't feel right for everyone, but try it. You may find the help you need.

Connect with others and turn your need into a way to help others. Try going out of your way to connect with old friendships that have slipped away. Try to contact those who are afraid to talk to you for whatever reason. Give them a chance to re-enter your friendship circle.

Look for commonalities with people you meet every day. You may find that you have something in common with the most unlikely people. Commonality brings instant connection. If you are introverted and have a hard time making early connections, gravitate towards an outgoing person and let THEM make the first step.

Become a listener. Ask questions and really care about the answers. Try a test run just once by asking questions of strangers you might meet casually during the day. Notice how people will open up to you if you care about them. This process will get easier and easier with practice.

Find your belayers. Think about who these people might be. Who would you throw the rope to? Talk to that person about the belay cues and how you could translate them to your situation. When you need someone to help you, this person will be ready.

Get rid of your poisonous friends. We all have those friends who sap us of energy and take too much. During transition, put these people in the outer circle. Take care of yourself, and surround yourself with YES people.

Identify your YES people. Go out of your way and establish a heart connection with some YES people. These are the unconditional friends who accept you as you are … and connect to your soul.

Think of the individuals you love to associate with. Notice the similarities between them. What does that tell you about how you want to be? Who you want to associate with? Who your encouragers are?

Identify your heroes. Put a picture of them somewhere so you can be reminded of someone who has inspired you. Sometimes this will spark you into the positive mode, and if you become negative, it will remind you that there is always a brass ring to reach for.

Don't give up. Make sure to look back and see how far you've come. Do whatever you have to do to make it to the peak. It will be hard, but you've made it this far, so use the help of others to make the final five percent.

Balance. Identify which parts of your life you neglected during your transition process.

Synchronicity. It happens and you don't even notice it sometimes. Think about the meaningful coincidences you have experienced. Make a list and you will see how lucky you are. The list will also help you notice when they happen.

Appreciate nature. Take long walks alone by the river, up the mountain, or in a quiet neighborhood. Walk slowly and take it all in. If you stop once in a while and look around, you may see the world of nature open up for you.

Think of your hero's journey. What have you learned? How have you changed? How will your experiences make your next journey different?

Serve others. Find ways you can serve others that are compatible with the skills you have learned along the way … or skills that may have been hidden that you can dig up … or skills you have honed all of your life.

About the Author

Cheryl Perlitz is best known for her insatiable spirit of adventure. Climbing mountains with backpacks, canoeing in the middle of nowhere, dogsledding in sub-zero conditions, rafting over waterfalls, and biking up and down the mountainside are her passions. After the death of her "adventure husband," both of her parents, and her dogs, she restructured her life and learned the true meaning of "climbing mountains." To Cheryl, the process of climbing a mountain is just like the process of managing the challenges we face every day of our lives.

Drawing on her experience as a small business owner, a mountain climber, an adventure trip leader, and an involved stay-at-home mom, Cheryl now facilitates inspiring workshops and seminars, and delivers motivating keynote speeches. She shares the lessons she has learned from the mountain to help others transform their own challenges at home and at work into opportunities for adventure and positive change.

Cheryl offers seminars and workshops to corporations and non-profit groups. For information on her interactive programs or to order books, contact her at: **www.SoarWithMe.com** or e-mail at cheryl@soarwithme.com.

Order Additional Copies

Toll-Free: 1-866-372-2636

Fax: 1-843-785-8722
secured online ordering
www.CameoPublications.com

	# Items	Amount
Soaring Through Setbacks: ***Rise Above Adversity*** ***Reclaim Your Life*** Cheryl Perlitz Paperback (ISBN : **$16.95**		

Shipping:
USA: $4.95 for first item;
add $2.00 for each additional book
SC residents please include 5% sales tax.

Order Total

Please Print

Name: _____

Company: _____

Address: _____

City: _____ State: _____ Zip: _____

Phone: (_____) _____

Cameo Publications, LLC
PO Box 8006
Hilton Head Island, SC 29938

Sorry no CODs

credit card # _____ expires _____

please sign _____